THE VANISHING PARSON

The Vanishing Parson

LAILE E. BARTLETT

Beacon Press

BOSTON

Grateful acknowledgement is made for use of excerpts from:

How to Become a Bishop Without Being Religious by Charles Merrill
Smith. Copyright © 1965 by Charles Merrill Smith. Reprinted by permission of Doubleday & Company, Inc.

Chapters I, II, IV, VII, and X from *Sex: Female; Religion: Catholic* by
Sally Cunneen. Copyright © 1968 by Sally Cunneen. Reprinted by
permission of Holt, Rinehart and Winston, Inc.

for
the parson
in my life

CONTENTS

Preface   ix

1   The Clergy Rebellion   1

2   Genesis of the Exodus: The Larger Context   19

3   Halfway Houses for Runaway Clergy   41

4   Second Oldest Profession   65

5   The Other Revolution   85

6   Holy Matrimony   109

7   The Case of the Vanishing Parson   137

8   The Called and the Calling   155

9   New Bells and New Bottles   185

Annotated Bibliography   223

PREFACE

Books by the yard have been written about the dying church, its fevers, and death rattle. Volumes more, about its growing irrelevance, about the tidal wave of alienated churchmen and defecting clergy, about the pressing need for rebirth and "renewal."

Most of these often scathing critiques are special pleading or the distilled cries of personal pain: the anguished bishop reliving and thereby relieving the trauma of his spiritual saga; the trembling headquarters executive devising a plan for shoring up the old structure, while the big money pulls out its foundation-stones; the radical theologian updating doctrine "in the light of current knowledge"; the nun finding "meaning" outside the cloister; the church statesman seeking to extricate his institution from the clutches of an even larger self-seeking establishment; the pastor striving for "relevance" in the ghetto; the seminary field-work man pressing for higher standards, as the students eagerly latch onto "new ministries"; the maverick preacher concocting new rituals with jazz and dance or exploring the secret passages of the "underground church"; the ex-priest daring to attack the sacred citadel of celibacy.

The time for diatribe and magnificent denunciation is past. Now the need is for a unifying perspective, a positive statement.

Apart from the special problems of Presbyterian and Jesuit, rector and rabbi, there are broader, overarching concerns.

Through all this confused, apparently aimless thrashing of religious institutions, there is a consistent theme and pattern. Its threads can be seen in the travails of the anxious clergy.

This book aims to trace the unifying theme through the many phases, forms, and digressions of the parson's troubled odyssey. More than that, it aims to look beyond to new patterns now taking shape, to the continuation of that theme in the freshness of bright green shoots already visible between the cracked grey building stones of the old sanctuaries.

Laile E. Bartlett
Berkeley, California

THE VANISHING PARSON

CHAPTER ONE

The Clergy Rebellion

BISHOP RESIGNS

MINISTERS MAN CITY HALL

MONSIGNOR MARRIES

EX-NUN COLLEGE PRESIDENT

CLERGYMAN TAKES GOVERNMENT POST

360 NUNS GO SECULAR

PRIEST RESIGNATIONS SOAR HERE

DISSIDENT CLERGY BLAMED FOR FUND SQUEEZE

First a trickle, then a torrent, then a tidal wave. The dam has broken. Priest and preacher, nun and rector, reverend and rabbi are unbuttoning the collar, kicking the habit, throwing in the stole.

What was once a quiet fade-out is now a noisy procession. The secret and furtive exit through the guarded back door has become a press conference with flashbulbs, out front. Dropout or prophet, rebel or zealot, they no longer tiptoe and whisper as they go.

But this much is clear: newsworthy though the string of defecting clerics may be, it is only one small thread

in a much larger skein, one theme in the intricate tapestry of
the institutional church, into which more than 126 million
American citizens and uncounted billions of dollars are tied.*

The church is in trouble—in crisis, and fighting for
its life. More than that, the shedding of the cloth is not even
the main issue in the momentous social upheaval, in which
the church is only a part.

What *is* happening to the church? To religion? How
can we get hold of fundamentals in a context so vast? Two
things we can do as a start:

1. Catalogue the complaints: Why *are* clergy leaving? What is their beef?
2. Make use of the clergy as a clue and an instrument: a weathervane to pick up the subtle nuances
and winds of change; a microcosm in which are concentrated the stresses and strains of the society at
large.

For what's eating the parson is what's eating everyone. Everyone is on a quest for meaning. But for the clergyman, whose *business* is meaning, the question is more pointed,
self-conscious and explicit, and the crisis more poignant.

This book will focus on him—the man in the middle,
the man caught at the vortex of anguish, change, and dilemma.

First, the Exodus . . .

Only a few short years ago, a brash churchman, here
and there, took a daring step and made headlines.

ITEM: William DuBay, white priest in a black ghetto
church, asked the Pope to fire his archbishop for his do-

* For information on statistics, sources, and references, see
annotated bibliography.

nothing policy on civil rights (*Life*, 1966). The archbishop promptly "broke" DuBay to a non-parish post.

ITEM: James A. Pike, thorn in the side of his church, renounced his post as bishop (1966), and explained it in a *Look* feature article. Later, he lashed out with another: "Why I'm Leaving the Church". (1969)

ITEM: President Jacqueline Grennan, a Sister of Loretto nun, asked that Catholic Webster College in St. Louis be turned over to a lay board of trustees and that she be released from her vows (1967). This was done. Soon thereafter she married a Jewish businessman.

ITEM: In a major cover story (1967) James Kavanaugh, a priest, blasted his church. Shortly afterward, he left. In 1968, he announced, "I'm glad I left."

Each such news item was avidly grabbed up by editors and as avidly devoured by the public. The combination was surefire: fame-plus-religion-plus-surprise-and-shock.

The formula still holds, but two things have changed: the departures are now fashionable, and the pace has increased.

Such news is now commonplace. And now, along with the headliners—Sister Mary Corita, or Bishop James Shannon—there are battalions of others. Announcements of wholesale defections, long lists like battle casualties, or statistics not bothering with names.

How many are leaving the church? There is no way of knowing exactly. Under the most stable of circumstances, church statistics are notoriously shaky. The *Yearbook of American Churches*, bible of denominational figures, patiently explains in each issue that its best figures are far from dependable. Churches don't even agree on a definition of who is a member. Some report only those who have been baptized; some, only adults; some include the whole cradle roll. More than this, not every church reports every year. So the actual total, for example, for 1969 is not really the nice, neat

128,469,636 that appears in print. Figures for some churches are more than a decade old.

To add to the confusion, some churches have a way of padding figures, even when things go well. When things go badly, who wants to advertise defections? Even if they try to be scrupulous, churches can't really know who's in or out. With twenty percent of American families moving every year, who knows for sure which signed-up members are still in town?

There are additional problems in trying to keep tabs on clergy. Many churches ordain for life. Their ministers who go into the real estate or bond business thus remain on the list. The American Baptists, we are told, and there are doubtless others, don't know how many ministers they have. A Catholic priest can take a leave of absence and then "jump the wall," not to return. As one priest commented, "People do not 'leave' the church any more. They are just suddenly not present."

But if churches are reluctant, or genuinely unable, to talk about leadership losses, there are plenty of other sources of information concerning the trend. Government agencies in Washington and elsewhere are aware of a significant influx of former clergymen. Within the Civil Service Commission, for example, there is a special committee to review applications of ex-clergy. The Office of Economic Opportunity has so many former parsons that it has been jestingly called the "Office of Ecclesiastical Opportunity."

The Michigan Civil Rights Commission not long ago counted twenty-two former clergymen on its staff. So many are now employed by San Francisco's city government as to have merited a newspaper feature article.

Schools and colleges, as always, are the haven for a great number of ex-pastors, but other agencies are now actively seeking out and cultivating those with ministerial experience.

The Commission on the Aging in Pennsylvania is reported to be impressed by the cleric's combination of pastoral interest, self-direction, and management ability as exactly right for certain posts. A California mental health agency is considering a special reorientation program to aid in recruiting clergy for new jobs opening up with them.

The *Gallagher President's Report*, a newsletter for executives, reported in 1969 that a leading management consulting firm was studying ex-clergy as a potential talent pool. An executive job placement firm, Earl Blue Associates, wrote to *Time:* "We especially concur with the comments you published concerning secular employment. The former clergymen we have placed are indeed highly qualified, and the jobs they obtain are an important part of the transition process."

A headquarters executive recently warned his denomination: "We should be aware that governmental agencies and businesses are presently actively recruiting former clergymen . . . [which] may have the effect of enticing more of the men who have not yet had the courage to take such action to do so. . . ."

One measure of the size and significance of the exodus is the burgeoning network of new agencies across the country designed to assist in the reorientation and placement of defecting priests, nuns, and pastors.* Many of these are delighted to report on their growing clientele. The Chicago branch office of Bearings for Re-establishment reported it had assisted 1,000 persons in twenty-one months. In 1968, Bearings in New York City headquarters worked with more than 2,100 clients and was in correspondence or conversation with 2,000 more.

In October, 1969, Bearings Director Patricia Allen

---

* See Chapter III for details on these agencies.

Roy reported that the various branches of that organization were giving service, in round numbers, as follows:

CITY	NUMBER PER MONTH
New York City	100–120
Austin, Texas	15 – 20
Miami, Florida	15 – 20
Washington, D.C.	40 – 50
Pittsburgh, Pa.	10 – 15
Buffalo, N.Y.	20 – 30
Toronto, Canada	30 – 35
Denver, Colo.	7 – 12
Chicago, Ill.	100
Los Angeles	80 –100

For March–April, 1969, Mrs. Roy estimated that nuns, priests, brothers, and pastors were leaving at the rate of *800 per month*, in the country as a whole. Eight hundred per month is a jolting figure, even if it can only be a conscientious guess. As Mrs. Roy says: "Any way you look at it, the number is large. And one can play games with it, because nobody really knows, and there may be no way to find out."

A San Francisco agency estimated that a total of 2,000 ex-nuns, priests, and pastors were living in that area in 1969. During 1968, there was a drop of 9,174 nuns (5.2%), almost double the largest previous decrease (1966). In 1969, the Vatican had on file more than 10,000 requests from various religious asking to be released from their vows. This is above the estimated further thousands who no longer bother to petition.

One Protestant denomination, also in 1969, discovered that, within the previous five-year period, *one-quarter* of all its active clergy had gone through one or more major "life-shifts," i.e., transfer out of the parish, leaving the ministry altogether, or divorce.

The Jesuits see manpower decreases in their provinces growing year by year. Fewer novices are entering, more seminarians are leaving, and priests, who rarely depart after ordination, now do so more and more. In the United States from 1965 to 1969 Jesuit ranks declined by 7.4%. Whereas seventy-six men left in 1965, by 1969 this number had grown almost fourfold: 281 taking their leave.

Meanwhile, an institution with few headlines and little fanfare about departures, the Union of American Hebrew Congregations, has commissioned a two-year study of the problems and changing directions among Reform rabbis.

Another index of defections is a growing network of ex-clergy counseling specialists. Dr. Angelo D'Agostino of Washington, D.C., is one of these. He is both a priest and a psychiatrist, having both professional skills and a helpful dual perspective. Another is Dr. Abraham Twerski of St. Francis General Hospital in Pittsburgh, an orthodox rabbi who is also a psychiatrist.

The seriousness of the clergy exodus is manifested in the proliferation of symposia and conferences on the subject. In May, 1969, the American Jewish Congress invited representatives of all branches of Judaism to a symposium to consider the disturbing and rising unrest among Jewish seminarians. In January, 1970, a conference on "The Shape of Clergy Restlessness" was sponsored jointly by the Boston Theological Institute and the Episcopal Theological School in Cambridge, Massachusetts. That same month, in Des Plaines, Illinois, a seminar was called by the Forest Hospital's Postgraduate Center for Mental Health on "Why Is the Clergy Leaving?" In February an ecumenical "Systems Conference" was held at Yale University, to which were invited representatives of all faiths and all components of the church system: seminary deans, seminarians, pastors, pastors' wives, ex-pastors, judicatory heads, seminary professors, to explore the implications of the newly released study, *Ex-Pastors: Why Men Leave the Parish Ministry* by the United Church of

Christ. Some of the data for this research was gathered at four regional conferences of ex-clergy, in Cleveland, Chicago, San Francisco, and New York. Shortly after, the Jesuit college invited its ex-clergy to gather on its Woodstock campus, to analyze and reassess implications of their new, outside-the-church status.

These examples do not include the many sessions of academic groups, such as the Society for the Scientific Study of Religion, the Religious Research Association, the American Sociological Association, and so on, where research papers on the topic are presented. Nor do they include the dozens of meetings and conferences sponsored by denominations themselves and by their concerned and threatened clergy associations.

In short, it is altogether clear that both men and women are leaving the church in growing numbers. More, in absolute figures, are leaving Catholic than Protestant bodies. But Protestant, Catholic, or Jewish—no religious institution is immune today.

Some religious professionals have always moved from the church to the secular world. There is no way of knowing how many. However, most observers agree that we are now witnessing "the most notable defection from the service of the church since the Reformation."

View from the Pew

The pulpit claims the headlines, but what of the pew? A sidelong glance at the mood and stance of the laity may lend perspective to an understanding of the clergy exodus.

ITEM: While pulpits empty, laymen leave, too. Church membership has declined, from 64.4% of the United States population in 1967 to 63.1% in 1969. More important than the change in this percentage is the reversal of a longtime trend: for the first time in recent years, church membership is *no longer keeping pace with*, much less keeping ahead of, the rate of population growth.

These overall figures do not apply to the conservative, ultra-conservative, or fundamentalist bodies. By contrast, these churches hold the line or show gains. Assembly of God, Southern Baptist, and Church of God, for example, report increases of various kinds. In January, 1969, the Church of the Nazarene showed gains in membership, denominational school enrollments and a record budget. Such statistics tend to average out, in the overall figure, the losses among Methodists, Lutherans, Presbyterians, and other "main line" churches.

ITEM: Church revenues are off. The Episcopalians, for example: their national staff in New York City was slashed by one-quarter in 1970. Their Board for Theological Education, "for financial reasons," recommended that denominational seminaries be reduced from eleven to five. In San Francisco, the bishop's mansion was put up for sale. The story is much the same for most "main line" bodies, as well as for their basket organization, the National Council of Churches, which in 1970 faced such declines in money and membership as to raise a basic question about its very existence.

Church construction is also sagging, steadily down from an all-time peak of $1.1 billion in 1966. Denominational publishing houses and seminaries are having red ink troubles, too.

ITEM: Change in public opinion may be most significant of all. There has been a right-about-face, say the polls, in people's view of the influence of religion. In 1957 Gallup reported that two-thirds of the men in the street believed that "religion was gaining in its influence in American life." By 1969, the opinion was just the reverse: only fourteen per-

cent thought so. The *Yearbook of American Churches* sin-
gled this out as "the most important religious development of
the decade."

The trend continues. By January, 1970, exactly three-
quarters of the public believed that the influence of religion
was on the decline. This, the Gallup Poll calls "one of the
most dramatic reversals of opinion in the history of polling."
For youth the figure is still higher: eighty-five percent of
them see religious influence as waning.

ITEM: Even the symbols are suffering a sea-change.
History tells us that whenever the holy becomes merely
quaint, the religion of a society is losing its grip. For some
years we have had cutie-pie Christ-childs on Christmas cards,
and crosses for earrings and costume jewelry. Now church
buildings as pleasure-domes enjoy a fad. A New York City
German Lutheran structure has become a discotheque. A
Baptist church in Amenia, New York, is now a supermarket.
In the refurbished Old Town section of Chicago, a former
Congregationalist chapel is now an art gallery and theater. A
former Episcopal sanctuary in Charleston, South Carolina,
ladles food as a restaurant. With a fine disregard for Jesus'
confrontation of the money-changers in the Temple, the
chapel at one financially distressed denominational headquarters was commandeered and cut up into cubicles for the fundraising department!

View from the Pulpit

For further perspective, one might check the mood
of those who stay, that is, the typical parish clergyman. First
of all, there is everywhere a new brand of restlessness and
activism. More and more parish ministers reveal increasing
anger and desperation as the Vietnam War drags on, and the
mood of the country builds into a full-scale "backlash." One
pastor wrote a colleague: "I wish I could see a clear highway

ahead—even a path—for rebel spirits such as we." Another confessed, if somewhat ungrammatically: "I'm reaching the point that if you want to be serious about social change you should get out of the church and get tied into the New Mobe or such."

These pastors identify in spirit with the Berrigans and William Sloane Coffins of the "new breed" of clergy, firebrands of social revolution, some of whom have suffered imprisonment, firing, even death for their witness. The "new breed" are found, however, overwhelmingly in campus ministries, in "new ministries" (to drug addicts, street people, etc.) or among seminarians, rather than the parish.

A minority among ministers has always associated itself with politics, pressure groups, and the social gospel. But today, demonstrations, processions, and symbolic acts are becoming standard items of the parson's tool kit.

How far this tendency has moved was shown recently at a staid pastors' conference on the West Coast. To be in tune with the times (1970) and to vent their frustration, they did something they had never done as a conference before: they organized a march! Some two hundred ministers, "mostly middle aged and quite respectable looking," said the press, ". . . marched in a general protest against human suffering."

Low risk causes such as civil rights or mental health or ecology are increasingly being supplemented by more daring ones. In many states clergy are involved in abortion referral agencies. Pastors also engage in such "treasonable" activities as providing sanctuary for draft resisters. Clergy and Laymen Concerned About Vietnam, which six years ago was a high risk venture for its clergy—founders, sends funds to Canada, where by 1970 more than 60,000 American men had fled to escape the draft.

A new sharp breeze is blowing, too, through clergy professional groups. The traditionally milquetoast ministers' association is becoming a union, with teeth. One pioneer in the change was William DuBay, who made waves a second time by daring to organize a priests' union in Los Angeles. This dramatic demand for "due process" did not get far. But the unheard-of issues it raised, such as clergy rights, contracts, and wages, are very much alive among Catholics.

The Association of Episcopal Clergy had picked up two hundred members by January, 1970. Other organizations, "union" in spirit if not in name, are forming among Lutherans, Methodists, Baptists, United Church, and other clergymen.

Scene at the Exits

Monitoring church exits will not give us much help in picking up the score. There are too many mixed signals, too many contradictions, as in each of the following:

1. *Who's Leaving Whom?* To hear some preachers tell it, they are leaving because the laity are "too stuffy, too complacent, too insensitive to vital issues, too stick-in-the-mud."

From three who have left:

[Laymen] tend to be too critical of the pastor and too uncritical of themselves . . . I am happy to be out of the parish trap.*

I felt I should move from the church because it seemed to be beset with smallness of purpose and out of touch with these times.

My first inclination is to say 'Go to hell!' . . . but that would be neither theologically sound nor

* For sources of quotations such as these, published and unpublished, see the annotated bibliography.

practical. There is a small concerned group left in the congregation—numbering perhaps three—and if I had any counsel for them it would be to get out, resign, and become active in the Democratic Party, the League of Women Voters, the poverty program . . .

Many social researchers agree. Says sociologist Jeffrey K. Hadden:

> The frustration and failure of most clergy to succeed in this task (of communicating their understanding of the meaning and implications of the Christian faith) have led many of them to withdraw . . .

But to hear many laymen tell it, *they* are the ones who are leaving! And the reason? Their *ministers* are too stuffy.

A Catholic lay worker at a conference asked: "How can we do any of these things when we can't even talk to our pastors?" A protestant layman at a conference on goals complained: "We want to move, but how can we get our two ministers off the dime?"

As for dull and uninspiring clergy: in response to a survey question "How would you evaluate the sermons in your parish?" over one half of the respondents in one inquiry checked "inadequate" or "poor."

A member of a lay group which broke off from a church summed it up: "Since we can't get together, we'll just go separately. Let the minister and his followers go their way, and we'll form a fellowship of our own."

2. *Push or Pull?* Scores of defectors do not hesitate to confess they wanted out:

Why I left?

A growing feeling of disenchantment with the church. A feeling church was "not where the action is."

Became tired of constant harassment and opposition from those in the church unwilling to let me do my own thing.

Became more and more impatient with petty administrative details (not enough secretarial help).

Disgust because I had to fight to do group programs, when outside groups asked me politely to do them and paid me besides.

Declares another: "The church primarily concerned with institutional maintenance and self-preservation is not worth trying to save. It is already dead."

But some of those milling outside the gates are outside against their will. When asked why he shifted out of the parish, one clergyman replied: " 'Shift'? What do you mean, 'shift'? I *was shifted!*" As two others explained:

After I was passed over for promotion enough times, I got the message.

I never wanted to be anything but a priest. My separation from the active ministry was unexpected and accompanied by bitter tears. Today I am laicized, a suspect of "heresy." But I still want to be a priest. Surely some day I'll be back.

Some firings make the news, like the noisy West Coast "busting" of William DuBay and the mass eviction of forty priests by Washington's Cardinal O'Boyle. The Washington priests had challenged the papal encyclical on birth control.

For every rabbi who has given up on his synagogue as "useless and obsolete" and left it voluntarily, there is another forced out, as eloquently reported in the spate of bestsellers about rabbis. Such was the fate of Arkady Leokum's protagonist in *The Temple,* and of Rabbi Gideon Abel in Herbert Tarr's *Heaven Help Us.*

3. *Too Fast or Too Slow?* Many agree with a rector in Chicago who said: "I'm getting out. There's no time to wait. We'll all be dead. The church is moving too *slowly.*"

Talk to a priest in New York and he'll sadly admit, for himself and others like him: "I'm sad to have to leave. I've kept my vows, but the church has not. It's changing too *fast.*"

4. *The Question of Authority?* One of the catchwords around the exits is "authority." There's no end of talk about "due process" and "top-down decisions," complaints about high-handed orders and rulings of bishops, boards, and presbyters:

> They bid you "follow the Lord," but if you step out of line—*Wow!*

> The tight bureaucracy at ———— headquarters makes its own rules, remote from the laity and the churches and the disinherited like myself.

From nuns in different parts of the country:

> When I left the Dominican order in 1961, after thirty years of trying to understand the great

Dominican motto of *Veritas*, I did so only because I *had* learned to live by it and could no longer go on living the mechanical robot (i.e. obedient) existence which religious life had become.

I know (obedience) should be helpful theoretically. Although there are opportunities to learn through concepts of obedience and authority, I have not yet been in any circumstances where I thought it could be lived in a mature way.

Authority would seem to be the key. But the authorities are leaving too! Bishop John (*Honest to God*) Robinson quit as Bishop of Woolwich, and accepted a college deanship at Cambridge. Bishop James P. Shannon, one-time chairman of the board of the Association of American Colleges resigned as auxiliary bishop of the Archdiocese of St. Paul–Minneapolis, two months after Pope Paul's 1968 encyclical against artificial birth control. He protested the necessity of keeping two sets of books as a bishop: "Privately believing one thing but having to teach another, I cannot in conscience give internal assent, much less external assent, to the papal teaching in question." He then went on to teach at St. John's College in Santa Fe, New Mexico.

5. *Leaving the Church?* "I want to forget the whole thing!" the ex-pastor in Texas exclaims with feeling. "It's like a bad dream—the mistake that I made. All those years that I gave, and wasted, in the ministry."

"Leaving the church? I'm more in the church now than I ever was," a New Jersey ex-pastor asserts. "Now I'm free to do the work of the church. I'm making up for the time I lost inside."

6. *Religious Fashions?* Even so mundane a matter as attire (how worldly can you get?) has become a battleground. In South Dartmouth, Massachusetts, three nuns were ordered back for reassignment after they had refused to wear religious habits at a parochial school. The school board of New Orleans, Louisiana, reversed itself and will allow a nun to wear her habit while teaching in a federally funded school program.

Father Arbuthnott, the spiritual adviser of the Roman Catholic seminary in Surrey, England, advised shedding the collar "when it might be an obstacle to pastoral contact," while the Pope instructed mother superiors "not to give in to the modern mentality" in dress.

Tailor and Cutter of London got into the act in 1968, suggesting that the cleric's wardrobe be livened with shirts and ties in matching colors:
—green for the long Trinity season
—red for Whitsun feast days
—purple for Advent and Lent
—gold for Easter and Christmas.
Nuns go high fashion; rosaries are set aside; priests turn their collars around—while the youth of the land take to robes, crosses, and beads, and a new batch of Protestants *starts* wearing clericals!

7. *"All for Love?"* "I left the church," says George Frein, "for love of Jeanne." Pages, reams, books, in the Roman Church at least, have been written about leaving the church "for love." Frein, now a professor at the University of North Dakota, admits quietly: "I left the church to marry Jeanne, because I loved her." It all seems so simple. But with Protestants, one finds another theme: "I left the church to divorce."

8. *And Back at the Seminary?* While enrollments at Protestant and Jewish seminaries are now on the rise, recruits at Catholic seminaries are falling off drastically. Though more students are entering Protestant and Jewish seminaries than ever before—the largest graduating class in the history of Hebrew Union College in Cincinnati, 1970—*a minority* of them say they plan to enter the *parish* ministry.

Of students at Union Theological Seminary in New York City, one of the largest and most prestigious of non-denominational schools, eighty percent said, in 1968, that they did not plan to go into parish work. At Yale, another leading divinity school, only seventeen percent were headed for the parish.

What are we to make of all this? Some say religion, the church, the ministry are all washed up.

But look around! Religion has never been more consistently in the forefront of the news. Its institutions may rock and reel, but religion itself has never been more vigorous or more lively.

CHAPTER TWO

Genesis of the Exodus
·The Larger Context·

What's *really* happening? One thing can be said: the trend of the moment is just the reverse of a decade ago.

In the 1950s, religion hit the jackpot. It was the age of the miraculous statistic: more members, more attending church, more religious best-sellers, more and bigger buildings and budgets, than ever before in history. Sixty-nine percent of the people believed that religion "was an increasing influence in American life." Sixty-two percent of the people belonged to some sort of religious organization. At no time in history, reported the editor of the *Yearbook of American Churches*, had such a great proportion of the American population been church members. It was assumed that, just as everyone had a shoe size, so he had a religion. Personal information forms routinely asked: "religious preference?"

It was agreed that religion was good for you, good for the country, good in the abstract. President Eisenhower counseled: "Go to church—*any* church—but go!"

Church historian Sidney Ahlstrom observed that in a country which has had its religion shaped by revivals, this revival was even more widespread, and "had at last engaged a significant number of first-rate intellectuals." It was so—for Protestants, Catholics, and Jews.

A summary of religion in America at the end of the decade confidently announced that the general upward trend "shows every sign of continuing."

Some scholars, however, sounded a note of caution. It was a boom in "religiosity" said they, not religion. More people joining the church? Yes. But more religious? No. More attending church? Yes. But what did they do when they got there? Held dances and raffles and played bingo. One observer called the great burst of piosity "the basket-ballization of the church"; another, the "peripheralization of religion." Beneath the sparkling surface, they warned of a strong undertow of science scouring away at the piers and pilings, the very abutments of religious faith.

The 1960's were something else. The happy graphs went limp; the statistics flattened and sagged. Suddenly, it was a time of hesitation, restlessness, and uncertainty.

It was a field day for the "God Is Dead" theologians, who tried to outshock each other with daring book titles like *Honest to God* and *For Christ's Sake*. They articulated the mood of mounting doubt: "Everything nailed down is coming loose." Religion, morals, national destiny, life itself—did these have ultimate meaning and goal? Few could say Yes.

The 1970's took off on a still different tack with: "The Church is dead!" As this decade opened, doubt deepened for many into despair, and a tired assortment of already outworn cliches: "the irrelevant church," "the obsolete synagogue," "the identity crisis of clergy/church/Christianity.

The recessional that wends its way from pulpit and chancel and out of the churchyard is not reassuring. Walt Whitman's words, "There will soon be no more priests," echoes in our ears. Comes the frightening whisper: "Not only the church, but religion, too, is dying."

While people were arguing, back in 1958, whether religion was approaching Heaven, or going to the dogs, sociologist Talcott Parsons declared that neither was true. Religion, said he, is neither dying nor reviving. Rather, it is being redistributed, rearranged, and redefined through the whole society and its culture.

Parsons was correct then, and what he said is even more true now. In ways we shall examine, often in ways not immediately recognizable as "religious," it is this restructuring and regrouping we see everywhere around us today, at many levels and on a monumental scale.

Our Peg—the Parson

Though for present purposes we have narrowed our field of vision from the impossibly broad sphere of religion in general to that of the parson, even he is no small peg to hang everything on. He's urban or suburban, sometimes rural, large church or small, liberal, radical, conservative, high church or low, eastern or western, midwestern or southern, Catholic, Jewish, any-branch Protestant, rabbi, pastor, or fifty-seven varieties of preacher and priest.

Why is he leaving? What book do you read? In *Why Priests Leave*, sharing "the intimate stories of twelve who did," Father John O'Brien of Notre Dame University gives his answer:

From a post-doctoral scholar at Yale: "Most priests leaving these days are doing so because they find life as a celibate having a crippling and destructive effect on their lives."

From a former Maryknoll seminary rector: "In examining my own reasons for leaving, I know that the major issue was celibacy."

From a former Jesuit priest, now a doctoral candidate at Columbia:

"Marriage was as much a part of my vocation as
was priesthood. For my own sake as well as for the
sake of others, I had to try to win a place for
married priests in the church . . . I simply believed
that it would be . . . for my own good and for
the good of the church if I asserted my desire to be
a married priest."

From a writer and scholar from England, now in
Chicago: "One of the most disturbing and revealing aspects
of the encyclical on priestly celibacy is the assumption that
a person can be conditioned or manipulated to fit painlessly
into the accepted model of priestly ministry."

From an associate in the development department of
the Illinois Institute of Technology: "All the love I gave or
received, for all the twenty-seven years of my previous state
of life, cannot equal or match the short year of love I have
found in a woman like JoAnne."

There are variations on the theme, to be sure, but the
thrust of Father O'Brien's book is that priests leave to live
and love as other men do.

In their book *Can These Bones Live?* two Methodist
journalists, former clergymen, point to the failure of programs of church renewal, as the source of disillusionment.
Robert S. Lecky and H. Elliott Wright see the "hope of the
world, namely the church" in dire need of transfusion and
revitalizing. But alas! the heralded programs and proposals
for renewal, which were, in turn, the "hope of the church,"
have failed. "Renewal" captured the focus of ecclesiastical
language as a fashion, they observe, but the bona fide field of
renewal "looks like the valley of dry bones in which the
prophet Ezekiel saw himself."

Professor Robert Katz of Hebrew Union College
says the rabbi wants to know whether there is a future for

him in a new society which is "rational, experimental, and nonparochial." Is there a place for the synagogue in a Jewish community replete with its own competing social welfare agencies, let alone the Community Chest and Red Cross?

Jeffrey K. Hadden spells out the parson's distress in *The Gathering Storm in the Churches*. To the "generation gap" and "credibility gap" he adds a "clergy–laity" gap.

This "widening gap between clergy and layman" is the parson's growing conviction that the aim of religion is to challenge social injustice, at the very moment his congregation wants most of all to be comforted. Because the preacher fails as a Moses to his stubborn "Hebrew children," he is withdrawing.

N. J. Demerath and Phillip E. Hammond observe that the parish may be a poor platform, anyway, for the man of prophetic bent. In their book, *Religion in Social Context*, they point out that the more radical and action-type clergy tend to be "siphoned off the parish structure, to avoid embarrassment and strained relations with parishioners."

Such pastors often "select themselves," for example, into campus work. There they don't have to answer to an up-tight board of deacons, or be confronted every Sunday by square people in square pews. There, they stand with the squares' sons and daughters, who are in revolt.

Thus, the anti-Vietnam firebrand, Daniel Berrigan, became a chaplain at Cornell University. Thus, too, the general HQ of the campus rebellion at San Francisco State College was the chaplains' Ecumenical House—until the church people who held its pursestrings shut it down.

Go to any religion conference to find your answer, and the reason for clergy restlessness will be summed up in one of two overworked words: "authority" or "relevance."

The monster "authority" seizes the clergyman from above and below. From his superiors—his bureaucracy, bishop, or judicatory—he is guided and pressured and confined. The nuns are ordered: Put on your habits and go back to work! Not only do the rebellious Dutch bishops get a flat NO on their celibacy petition, but are told: From now on you'll take vows every year.

Said a United Church of Christ pastor: "Conference executives have power of professional life or death (over us) . . . absolutely no accountability to anyone in their exercise of this power . . . In case of problems . . . they throw the minister to the wolves. . . ."

Recalled a Benedictine priest: "I was called in and sternly rebuked for having brought up such 'controversial' questions, and warned not to mention the war again. [Later] I was summarily forbidden ever to preach again."

And another: "No seminary training of mine ever dealt squarely with the problem of [clergy] who are unjustly rejected by church authorities. . . ."

But it is the parishioners in most churches—even in the more rigidly structured ones—who really have the last word. The church is a voluntary association. The laity can close it down in a hurry, by sitting on their pocketbooks or walking out. Moreover, in many denominations, the local congregation has explicit power to hire and fire the minister. All these pressures are operating. In recent months the results are highly visible in declining rosters and budgets.

"Relevance" is the other specter which hangs over the man in the meaning business. When his task is unrelated to the meanings and lives of people, his *raison d'être* evaporates. James Gustafson tells of a suburbanite pastor driven to riding the 8:07 in order to "relate" to his commuter flock by dealing himself a hand of bridge.

How relevant is the rabbi, asks Professor Katz, to a society impatient with the past, when his basic claim to being heard lies in interpreting classic Jewish tradition? Who needs him, now that Jewish and American identification are so compatible? when so many Jews nominally affiliate with the synagogue and so few take part in its worship?

Why is the clergyman leaving?

In order to marry?
The failure of renewal?
The loss of clear function?
Estrangement from the laity?
To be free to speak out?
The pressures of authority?
A sense of irrelevance?

One or more of these reasons may force him to leave, but underlying all is one basic and encompassing issue: *the quest for personhood.* It touches layman and cleric alike. For the parson's people and himself, this is the issue around which all others revolve. He is restless. He is leaving because the ministry as he finds it, fails to fulfill his own personhood, and blocks his efforts to help others be persons.

Collision Course

Two forces have been building up in our culture for a great many years: two mighty streams which meet and clash and, in the end, will have to blend. They are qualitatively different, but equally insistent.

The one is technological; it has to do with knowledge, invention, exploration, techniques. The other is essentially religious—a matter of meanings and understandings, purposes, humanness, and relationships.

Technology has brought us lasers and quasars, computers and multimedia, the telescoping of time and space, the SST.

The other force brings the new technology into question. It asks, What for? Now we are face to face with man the slave of his own machines, man the bumbling wrecker of his planet and his species, man the moral animal who must somehow learn to manage the knowledge he has for life rather than for death.

The two clash everywhere. One sphere of conflict, a present and raging example, not unrelated to the current turmoil in pulpit and pew, is the confusing world of sex. Here the technological revolution has delivered a department store of gimmicks, inventions, and know-how, focusing on birth control, abortion, and increased physical enjoyment. It has also created the media and means for distributing these throughout society and across the levels of age and class. Pills, loops, and foam are subjects of daily conversation; preparations delicately advertised in former days as for "feminine hygiene" are now boldly purveyed in ice-cream flavors. Reuben's *Everything You Always Wanted to Know About Sex* goes on the how-to shelf along with Spock's *Baby and Child Care* and Rombauer's *Joy of Cooking*.

Here, also, the meaning-revolution steps in to ask, What goes on? What of love and life and meaning, in today's context of techniques and expertise? It steps in, as well, to challenge yesterday's meanings. Bringing new understandings of human worth and personal fulfillment, it looks anew at birth and death. To deal with birth control and abortion is to deal with life and death. It brings new understandings of human sexuality and human potential, glimpses of new possibilities in human relating. A hundred new "Esalens" offer new worlds of touching and feeling and consciousness. Five hundred communes from Amana to Zion City are out to build post-revolutionary society right now.

So it must all be sorted out—the technical and the spiritual, the present and the past.

The ferment comes to a boil in the church in a dozen passionate controversies, engaging preacher, parishioner, progeny, and Pope. On the brink of explosion is the unholy trinity, the ABC's of sex: abortion, birth control, and celibacy.

Of celibacy, the pontiff of *aggiornamento*, John XXIII, said in 1960:

> we are grieved to see that some . . . manage to
> think that the Catholic Church will come to
> renounce, on principle or from expediency,
> something which . . . still is one of the most
> noble and pure glories of its priesthood.

His successor says he intends "to leave celibacy in its intact beauty." The Pope seems to feel that the destruction of religion is at stake; the clergy see the issue as denial of their right to be fully human.

The "personhood revolution" is shaking foundations in the church and everywhere today. This revolution took place, in theory, a long time ago: in the 1700's, as the flowering of the Enlightenment. First articulated in elegant drawing rooms and paneled libraries and for centuries limited in practice only to some of the people, now this ultimate acceptance of genuine democracy is everywhere, not just horizontally but vertically, straight down through the layers of this "classless" society.

Its gospel says that what matters most on this planet is the human person; that anything which hurts or harms or impinges on his health and welfare and fullness of being is wrong. It says that in the few short years he has on this earth, each human being should have the right to develop the only real thing he has: his self, and that this self has a potential of undreamed-of possibilities.

The gospel of personhood is moving in where the church creeds once lived. It is moving to the pulpit, the parsonage, the pew. In so doing, it precipitates a first-magnitude crisis of belief.

The "Crisis of Belief"

Some have always doubted their faith, but these have been the exceptions, the heretics. Now, most of the people are heretics! The key tenets of church creeds are no longer held by the majority of Americans. One recent study came up with these figures:

Only forty-one percent of United Church members "know God really exists"; only thirty-six percent believe in life after death. Only thirty-four percent of Methodists and thirty-nine percent of Episcopalians believe in the Virgin Birth. Only twenty-two percent of Methodists, thirty percent of Episcopalians and thirty-five percent of Presbyterians think man is a sinner. These figures are from Charles Y. Glock and Rodney Stark's *Religion and Society in Tension*.

Unbelief is so widespread among the "faithful" that it begins to be a question of who's kidding whom. Other research suggests that the clergy have no more, probably even less, confidence in the "belief" package they're selling than the parishioners who buy it! Twenty-six percent of the clergy, in one study, were found to be doubtful about the miraculous birth of Jesus; eighteen percent, skeptical about the doctrine of divine judgment after death. Sixty-two percent of the clergy say they would *expect* a thinking Christian to have doubts about the existence of God.

Furthermore, there is nothing even approaching unanimity on such articles of faith as belief in God, divinity of Christ, biblical miracles, life after death, and so on, either among denominations or within them.

Why the growing skepticism? In the words of one researcher: simply because the articles of religious faith "are no longer plausible in the modern world."

The result, he and others find, is that religion has become "privatized." That is, what one personally accepts has become more important than what the church wants one to accept.

"Simple, unreflective, knee-jerk affirmations—such as 'I believe in God/Revelation/Messiah'—have no future," says Jacob Neusner of contemporary Judaism. He predicts:

> Either people will figure out what they are saying
> when they use religious language . . . or they
> will stop using it. For the young people, in
> particular, there is no need to say the words
> —religious 'politeness noises'—they think their
> parents want to hear. Society has dropped
> conventional religiosity.

From one angle, the crisis of belief can be viewed hopefully as the prelude to a total rethinking of religion. But for the institution, such rethinking may mean dissolution. In point of fact, the process is just beginning. The unhinging of personal beliefs, which so terrifies some, has rippled only the surface of the broad and deep ocean of organized religion in America. These are only the waves; the deep waters beneath are not yet astir.

There are hundreds, even thousands, of congregations—whatever the questions of individual members—in which the institutional glue still holds and it is "business as usual." Drop into a dozen churches in any town or suburb: no problem—the form is not changed, the words are the same. The dutiful attendants fill the pews, pass the plate, recite the creed, sing the old hymns. They read the scripture, confess sinfulness, ask divine help. They smile Sunday smiles, welcome new members, and, before they go home, press the parson's hand at the door.

Especially is this true in the right-wing churches. There is no rain on their Sunday picnic, no crisis of belief or structure, for they, by definition, are committed to literalism, separatism, and personal salvation apart from society. Their happy statistics, the outstanding exception in the 1960's, prove it. The decade 1959–1969 was in every respect one of "outstanding growth"—more money, more members, more colleges, for churches like the Nazarene.

This book is about the storm at the top. Only a few, at the moment, feel the wind, taste the salt, fear the swell and the spray. Only a few sense the urgency, the institutional consequences of what are now only largely individual uncertainties. But even for these, it is not all alike. Some are quite consciously trying to ride out the storm, hoping the winds will die and the waves subside. Some shore up seawalls or frantically put their fingers in the dike, against the rising waters. Some themselves do battle, throwing their ecclesiastical weight around, sounding their bullhorns through the din.

Some listen to the waves, to catch what they are saying. Some ride with them, casting themselves on the mercy of the sea. Some, with Bishop Pike, jump ship. But most of those caught in the squall are frightened by the might of the blow, frightened even more by their own bewilderment and helplessness.

On closer inspection, the current "crisis" is not loss of belief, nonfaith or even unbelief, but, rather, a different belief: one that is different from the "old time religion" of assertions and promises. The new Credo, which supplants and displaces the old, has nothing to do with biblical authority, original sin or the Trinity, the Resurrection or divinity of Christ, but with personhood.

Moreover, the new faith with its personhood gospel comes not from the church and its pronouncements, but from the world of reason and science, education, government, and "causes." It, too, has its saints and its prophets: Thomas Jefferson and Thomas Paine, Albert Camus and Albert Schweitzer, Martin Buber and Martin Luther King.

And it has, for some today: Joan Baez, Herbert Marcuse, LeRoi Jones, Eldridge Cleaver. It has its scriptures and its working papers: the Bill of Rights and Constitution, petitions and reform laws, Supreme Court rulings and Robert's Rules, and more coming: from e. e. cummings and Hesse, Baldwin and Schutz, Malcolm Boyd, and the *Whole Earth Catalog*.

This is the non-church religion, the working religion, the consensual religion, as opposed to the bits and pieces of creedal religion stored away in the separate and peripheral boxes of the churches.

Part of the crisis of belief, for the churches and their seminaries at least, is that the new gospel comes not from traditional scriptures, but from outside. They too must turn to the world, therefore, in their quest for "relevance."

Part of the crisis is that the new faith is spreading to the despised and rejected of the earth: to the blacks—to the bottled-up, stifled, manipulated blacks, who have at last taken to heart as real for them the gospel of personhood. It is spreading peacefully, and violently—with the Martin Luther Kings, the Malcolm X's, and the Panthers. It is spreading to the Puerto Ricans and Chicanos, the Young Lords of Harlem, the grape-workers of the California Central Valley. It is spreading to youth on the streets, in the ghetto, on the campus, in the military. Youth marching, dancing, carrying signs, strewing flowers, wearing beads, "blowing" pot. It is spreading to women, suddenly standing up and saying they mean to be persons, not second-class citizens, from now on.

It is even spreading to the church!

This is hardly to say that brotherhood and care for others are exactly new to the church. Historically it claims to have originated them. All are woven through the scriptures and teachings of the major religions from the beginning. But these have not been the rock on which the cathedrals have been built, or the dogma on which the multitudes have taken their stand. Rather, the churches have consistently found ways to stone their prophets and to ignore or circumvent these human concerns.

Social research is beginning to document this standing complaint with the shocking finding that "the religiously devout are, on the average, more bigoted, more authoritarian, more dogmatic, and more anti-humanitarian than the less devout."

From their research, Glock and Stark report this correlation: "Those who believe the most doctrines and attend church the most often are, by and large, the ones less interested in ethical concerns." In short: "members of Christian churches in this country are on the average more bigoted than non-churchgoers."

The Crisis of Structure

Along with rising uncertainties about matters of doctrine, there is, to put it bluntly, a first-rate crisis of faith in the institution itself.

How can an institution founded on the rock of a particular and "eternal" creed or belief, survive when that belief is thrown into question, or another put in its place? How does a church admit it was wrong about "eternal verities," its truth, "God's truth"? How can people believe again when the "infallible" becomes fallible?

How can the church handle change in so changeless and fundamental a matter as the belief-structure on which it has staked its existence? How can it, if it would, clear the decks to make way for another creed? Even if the church confesses error, how can people now schooled in process—scientific and democratic—ever again accept ready-made truth handed down from above?

In this latter regard, at least, the nondogmatic, creedless churches fare better. They never claimed finality or ultimate truth, and so are not caught in this particular bind. To the extent that they have kept their vows to remain genuinely open, they will now be spared this agony.

As the new faith in the potential of persons washes in over churches everywhere, over churches founded by Wesley or Knox, Luther or Fox, how does it speak to their denominational boundaries, their divisions, their long protected separateness?

The new faith applies equally to Catholics and Humanists, rich and poor, old and young. It blurs, even erases, the lines between Catholic and Jew and Protestant, church and anti-church. In the new context, brand-names appear to be structural hangups: not just Methodist, Baptist, Jewish, Presbyterian, but American Baptist (that's northern), African Methodist Episcopal (that's black), Reform Jewish (that's liberal).

But they are stuck with the brands and the walls that shut in their empires. How many billions are invested in patching and perpetuating their separate institutional identity? In seminaries which are *per se* Episcopalian, Jesuit, or Southern Baptist? In Lutheran and Presbyterian office buildings? In whole systems of parochial schools? Religious orders, denominational publishing houses, separate and distinct mission programs at home and abroad?

Will ecumenism wipe out the offending divisions, or invent ways of cooperation and consolidation to save the day?

Certainly merger is in fashion: Congregational Christian with Evangelical and Reformed, United Methodist with Evangelical United Brethren, carrying to greater heights the unions of an earlier day.

And now, proposals for the Merger Supreme: the huge and unprecedented "COCU" plan to merge nine great Protestant denominations into one big "Church of Christ Uniting": The United Methodists, United Presbyterians,

Presbyterians U.S.A., United Church of Christ, Christian (Disciples), African Methodist Episcopal Zion, African Methodist Episcopal, and Christian Methodist Episcopal Church.

A church of twenty-five million parishioners! A third of the Protestants in the land!

The panacea, Ecumenism, moves in other ways, too:

> Denominational seminaries forming ecumenical clusters
>
> Seminary clusters joining in cooperative programs with universities
>
> Catholic and Protestant women organizing the Women's Ecumenical Liaison Group
>
> Orthodox and Roman Catholics agreeing on theology of Holy Communion
>
> even the United States Navy christening a "kosher destroyer," manned by Protestants: the U.S.S. *Bronstein*, flying Jewish insignia.

Even greater consolidation is foreshadowed, if not envisioned, in talk and titles: "Dying Denominationalism," "The End of Denominationalism," and "Denominationalism —an Era that is Past."

The Ecumenical Fallacy

However, there are as many factors working against ecumenism as for it. Before taking out membership in the Amalgamated Church of Tomorrow, one should take account of them. Not the least is denominational inertia. The spirit of ecumenism, in principle, may have overcome this, but long tradition and firm patterns die hard—to say nothing of investments. One newsman who studied the matter for ten years tagged the Vatican's portfolio at five billion dollars. In July, 1970, the Holy See published a denial of what it called "simply fantastic" reports, some ranging up to thirteen billions.

Yet whatever billions of dollars are invested in the maintenance of separate churches, the investments of human beings count for more, practically, in terms of ecclesiastical posts, established careers and prestige. Battle lines and resistive strategies are being developed by threatened church personnel, with types and degrees of acceptable cooperation being carefully assessed and planned.

Some "cooperative ventures" much publicized as ecumenical are, in fact, mere strategies preferable to even more threatening partnerships and mergers. One plausible reading of the new "cooperative" alliances among ultra-conservatives is, a united front against the liberal threat.

Mergers are not necessarily motivated by ecumenical high-minded altruism. "It could not have been altogether for love of John Wesley," Lecky and Wright point out in *Can These Bones Live?*, "that the less than one million member Evangelical United Brethren denomination permitted itself in 1968 to be fed into the yawning mouth of its enormous and topheavy Methodist sister. Rumors were that impending E.U.B. membership and financial problems floated away as easily as identity, once merged."

Seminary clusterings, likewise, are often dictated more by the dwindling strength and attractiveness of even the largest seminaries, when compared to the universities. To survive at all they have to pool resources. As seminary clustering takes place, the moving of religion, as subject matter, out of the seminaries and into the university itself, may be taking place even faster.

The most significant factor blocking a "mighty ecumenical Christian Church," however, is of quite a different order. In actuality, denominations are falling apart internally faster than ecumenism can get them together. Cracks and cleavages are appearing in all churches. Differences between Methodist and Methodist, Catholic and Catholic, are becoming greater than those between Methodist and Catholic. The new cleavages are of two kinds, growing deeper every day, and they are polar in nature. Some relate to religious *belief;* others to religious *relevance.*

Belief issues today are different from and more critical than the perennial, one might say normal or even healthy, debates over doctrine. They are, rather, as delineated by Glock and Stark:

> Not whether the bread and wine of communion
> become the actual blood and body of Christ
> through transubstantiation . . . but whether or
> not Jesus was merely a man. . . . Not how to
> worship God properly but whether or not there is
> a God of the sort that makes any sense to worship.

The other polarization, "the gathering storm in the churches," is the crisis of social relevance. Liberal clergy and laity are walking out on a church that is irrelevant. These people have moved beyond the issue of belief.

For millions of others, however, the irrelevance of the church *is* its relevance! For the vast majority, it is a bulwark of the unchanging and secure in a fearfully changing and insecure world. Its very removal from social controversy —its acceptance of, conservation of, prevailing social values— is its reason for being.

The church is an extremely conservative institution. There is no debate about this. The question is: what *should* it be doing? Attacking the ills of the world? Or standing aloof from them? And here, the churches are splitting down the middle into no-compromise camps.

What does this fundamental and widening polarization mean for the one, great, happy, inclusive church of the future? Some see, rather than such a church, the start of "a new denominationalism," far more divided in belief and commitment than any known in the past. Some see the divisions already so deep and entrenched as to make accommodation within one structure, old or new, impossible.

As for the "church of the future," a consultant to the National Council of Churches, Robert Duggan, makes this prediction: "If this new church has any one sign, it is pluriformity, diversity . . ." He notes that a study for the American Catholic Bishops came up with fifteen different and distinct conceptions of ministry prevalent in the American church today. "Such divisions are not theoretical, not bureaucratic. They exist in people who are the congregations."

Thus the hopes and dreams of an ultimate church union may have their roots in the soil of an ecumenical fallacy. This delusion is that one can succeed with bigger and bigger mergers of bigger and bigger structures. While one has his eye on the One Great Merger, the components may be falling apart, their juices evaporating. The ecumenical game may end with a vast assemblage of ecclesiastical shells from which most of the meaning and vitality has vanished, leaving standing an empty monument to a least-common-denominator "faith."

The Matter of Machinery

It is the nature of institutions to grow until the aims with which they started are forgotten, and their machinery is too complex and unwieldy to do their job. So with the church. Protestants like to think of the Roman Catholic Church in such terms, as a monstrosity, and themselves, by contrast, as simply "congregational" or "episcopal" or "presbyterian" in form of organization ("polity").

All churches have evolved into bureaucracies: centralized, hierarchical, and complex. Whatever their "polity" or brand of theology, as Paul Harrison has noted, all of them operate in much the same way. Whatever their rationale, they tend to move in the same direction and to become more alike: big, centralized bureaucracies.

The reasons are twofold, and quite simple. Once an organization gets rolling, it is hard to stop. Understandably, the persons who run it get attached to it, and want it to succeed, which in turn becomes the Goal. Moreover, the bureaucratic method is the most efficient way to run an institution, especially a large one or one that is growing. The super-bureaucratic Roman Catholic Church ranks very high in organizational efficiency. Not long ago a management firm rated it eighty-eight percent efficient on its scale. An excellent score for any institution, remarkable for a church.

Bureaucracy is, in mass society, a necessary form of organization. At best, it is a way of making sure everyone is included and is given equal treatment.

But at the same time, this treatment—like the computers on which today's bureaucracies depend—is mechanized, impersonal, and programmed to goals built rigidly into the structure. All this is very difficult to change—like trying to get your mixed-up magazine subscription straightened out with the company's computer. To change some of its goals, the whole mighty complex would have to be changed.

This is where the churches are today. Not only does the church bureaucracy find it difficult, in the maze of machinery and assignments, to remember its goals (in *practice*, not in rhetoric!) but it is unable to carry them out.

Thus, if the message of our time is "personhood,"

demanding sensitivity to and radical criticism of human behavior, the institutional church finds itself locked into an
impersonal status quo mode, reinforced by its status quo
middle-class membership as against the rest of society.

Again, if an aim of the church is community, its people craving warmth and genuine care, what good is an institution so big that it is cold and formal? "You can't have an
agape with 1,500 people" a longing housewife complained.

"Sometimes I feel the Mass would really mean something," another wistfully volunteered, "if it were celebrated
at home among friends." (Shades of John Wesley, who built
Methodism on small "classes"!)

The crisis of structure, in short, is the churches' own
topheaviness. As Reuel Howe puts it, "They've overstaffed
the barracks." They've removed it from "where it's at" with
people and issues. Their worst enemy is not their critics but
themselves. They are ripe for "purification," the back-to-
fundamentals pendulum-swing that was bound to come.

Up to now institutional churches have had the power
to resist such demands. They have had enough hold over their
members to vest in officials the prerogative of speaking for
the church and to interpret scripture, devise and execute
policy. In all this the Church of Rome has been the classic
case and master. It has managed to contain, surround, and
finally absorb, dissident groups and rebel sects.

Thus it contained St. Francis's order. Francis, the
mediaeval apostle to the urban poor, died disappointed to see
what had been made of the "lengthened shadow" of himself.
Today he must smile to see his remote devotees, the Franciscans, leave their comfortable and beautiful Santa Barbara
Mission to work in Oakland's ghetto.

With its vast inheritance of wealth and power and
machinery, the Church of Rome is today the most vulnerable
of all to the pendulum-swing reaction.

There is both glory and irony in the fact that it was

Rome's own lord and prince of churchly empire, Pope John XXIII, who in all his pomp, jewels, and robes opened the floodgates with Vatican II.

It is ironic, too, that the Protestants, no less than the Catholics, are both victims and beneficiaries of this unparalleled event.

CHAPTER THREE

Halfway Houses for Runaway clergy

She sat there in the outer office, in an ill-fitting, rumpled suit and shapeless coat—eyes averted, white knuckles clutching a lumpy string bag. The agency director, passing by, took note and said to her assistant: "Have we got a sandwich or a piece of cake from last night?"

Hungry she was: a runaway nun, it turned out, who had spent nine days and nights on benches in Grand Central station. She had existed on a can of Metrecal a day.

"I couldn't go back. There's no place to go. My family—now my parents won't talk to me. Last night—it was about three A.M., I guess—a priest came by. He told me about you. Can you help?"

Leaving the church is a terrible ordeal, an uprooting of everything. It's like leaving your wife, and for most, a very last resort.

One priest recalls: "The decision was the most difficult I had ever made. I had to convince myself that I was losing neither my faith nor my mind in asking hitherto unthinkable questions."

Career consultant Robert G. Dease says that his ex-clergy clients take an average of twenty-three months to make their decision. Priests like those in John O'Brien's book, *Why Priests Leave*, wrestled with the problem much longer. Father Eugene Schallert, sociologist at the University of San Francisco, found that his respondents took four to five years. So did those in the 1969 United Church of Christ study, *Ex-Pastors*.

When the clergyman finally takes the plunge, there is a new set of hurdles staring him in the face: moving into the marketplace, competing for a job, learning to live with his decision. His needs are many, his assignment awesome.

Lifeboats to the Rescue

A whole network of agencies has sprung up from no-where to meet the ex-pastor's needs.* Individuals and firms with high-sounding names beckon him from the Yellow Pages, call out from the classified ads.

Some of these are not addressed to clergy in particular:

VOCATIONAL COUNSELING ASSOCIATES: Personnel Evaluation–Aptitude Testing.

XYZ PERSONNEL SERVICE AGENCY: Permanent or Temporary Executive Professional and Technical; Professionally Directed Testing Program.

Some speak directly to his condition:

LOOK BEFORE YOU LEAP (LEAVE): EARL BLUE ASSOCIATES.

* For more detailed information on these, see annotated bibliography.

NEXT STEP: Assistance in transition from religious to lay state. Ecumenical, weekly open house; employment and other contacts.

PRIESTS ARE EXECUTIVES. Priests changing careers are like the many executives we consult daily. Dissatisfied with present high-level positions? Unsure about finding something new? Our executive consultants can help. HUMAN RESOURCE DEVELOPERS.

FOUNDATION FOR RELIGIOUS TRANSITION, Professional Refocus Operation, Santa Barbara, California, offers to religious professionals these fall programs: clergy conferences for clergy who wish to reevaluate their institutional service. Fall Session for six weeks: clergy and laity in religious transition.

Almost overnight, they have spread across the map. To name a few:

Chicago (with branches in Minneapolis, Boston, and San Francisco): HUMAN RESOURCE DEVELOPERS

Washington, D.C.: Bernard Haldane's CAREER FOCUS PROGRAM and John Mulholland's CAREER PLANNING INSTITUTE

Los Angeles: ROBERT G. DEASE ASSOCIATES, and TRANSITIONAL RESOURCES, INCORPORATED

New York City: BEARINGS FOR RE-ESTABLISHMENT, INC., with connections overseas and a scattering of branches from Texas to Toronto

San Francisco: EARL BLUE ASSOCIATES, expanding

to Honolulu and Texas, and NEXT STEP, setting up agents in Sacramento, San Jose, San Diego, and Denver.

Detroit: headquarters for CONTACT, also expanding.

And how many others, like the RESOURCES CENTER FOR PARISH CLERGY in Lubbock, Texas, were designed and planned but never got off the ground?

The Market

Will there continue to be enough customers for this burgeoning industry? From every indication, there are plenty more where these ex-clergy came from, ready and waiting in the wings. The comprehensive and definitive 1970 Episcopal study of their active clergymen declared: "One half of parish priests seriously have considered or are presently considering leaving the ministry. Thirty-eight percent would like to move to another parish."

One 1969 study compared samples of pastors who had left and those still "in." It found that at least a quarter of those still "in" disclosed deep uncertainty and restlessness. In interviews, they volunteered serious personal doubts as to whether they should continue with their church, marriage, or both.

One agency director says: " 'Why not call it quits?' is a question just about every parish clergyman has entertained at one time or another." And the United Church *Ex-Pastors* study concludes: "The greatest significance of this study may not be in the consideration of those who have already left the pastorate, but rather in the question of how many are thinking about leaving. . . ."

Many of those manning the lifeboat agencies were once parish clergy themselves. Professional Refocus Operation in Santa Barbara is the brainchild of ex-Episcopal rector John Wesley Downing and the late James A. Pike. Pike's story is well known: five headlined years of "heresy" trials, a hassle over his divorce and remarriage, then the decision to leave, triggered by what he denounced as the church's "performance gap." And finally, his dramatic death in the Holy Land.

Graduate of an Episcopal seminary, John Downing held, for ten years, a string of pastorates, resigning in 1968. Then, while teaching in Eureka, California, he hit on the idea of assisting "restless clergy who drop out—and *in* to greater community service."

In March, 1969, he and Pike brainstormed the idea for "new professions and credentials for clergy on the move." Two weeks later he had moved his family to Santa Barbara. "We have a tent that folds easily," he said.

Donald Winter, program director for Robert G. Dease Associates in Los Angeles, the firm whose clergy-help arm is Transitional Resources, Incorporated, is a young United Church of Christ ex-pastor. He graduated from Harvard Divinity School, went to a cooperative ministry in Chicago, there enrolling in a program of community renewal training, and returned to his native Los Angeles where he wound up in rehabilitation work. He first heard of Dease at a Bearings meeting. It struck him that Dease's approach, developed with executives, ought to work also for skid-row derelicts. He talked his agency into trying a pilot run using the Dease method. It was a great success.

Though now carried on by others, Bearings for Reestablishment, Inc. was founded by William P. Restivo, a priest who had come from an African missionary assignment to New York City. Appalled at the rejection of ex-clergy, he decided to help others who, like himself, had defected.

Warren Barker, the volunteer head of Bearings' branch in Washington, D.C., was formerly dean and psy-

chologist at Loyola University in New Orleans. John Mulholland, director of the Career Programming Institute, Inc.,
in Washington, though never ordained, was in training for
the priesthood for thirteen years.

Father David Sass, director of development of Next
Step, was a graduate of the Church Divinity School of the
Pacific (Episcopal). He served several parishes, the decisive
one being St. Edmund's in the Bronx, where he tasted life in
the ghetto. He worked with a fighting street gang, "The
Innocents," and became involved in the struggle to help hospital workers secure union-scale pay. When he issued a statement supporting the workers, he was reprimanded by his
superiors. It was then that he discovered that "the church is
not in touch with the blood-and-guts people I lived with for
twenty-four hours a day. The bishop should have lived on
my street."

Cele Caestecker, executive director of Next Step,
was for eighteen years a teaching nun in the Order of the
Sacred Heart. She left in 1967, when she was an assistant
professor of English and freshman dean at Barat College,
Lake Forest, Illinois. She and Nina Seawick, a former missionary nun, started *Next Step* in a private house in Menlo
Park, near Palo Alto, for others having trouble taking "the
next step" to secular life. They held regular "at homes."
News of their work spread by word of mouth. Soon David
Sass joined them. The enterprise then moved to San Francisco, finding a sympathetic landlord in Humanist House,
until they acquired quarters of their own.

Ed Krzyzewski made as dramatic a switch as one can
imagine. He was a Primitive Benedictine priest, a founder–
member of their monastery near Big Sur, California. There,
for the "highest order of sanctity" the rule is one even more
strict than that of the Trappists. Some live in absolute isolation and silence. Today, he is personnel director of Bearings'

busy headquarters office in the hurly-burly of New York City.

Human Resource Developers' chief, Dean Dauw of Chicago, was a Catholic priest. Its Boston office is headed by James L. Lowery, Jr., an Episcopal priest in good standing and a secretary of the Association of Episcopal Clergy.

Though Catholics furnished the impetus for the largest ex-clergy agencies, such as Bearings and Next Step, these undertakings are thoroughly ecumenical in spirit and fact. New York City's Bearings estimates its clients are now twenty-five percent Protestant, and it has helped a dozen rabbis.

For those who are mystified by the hundreds of clergy who simply "disappear," here then is one clue to where at least some of them surface: helping others like them through the gates. Of course, a mystery remains: why, if they have left the ministry, do they turn right around and spend their time, their whole life in some cases, with the clergy?

Business or Charity?

There are two kinds of agencies assisting former clergy. One is a business operation, the other, social service. The first sees ex-clergy primarily as an exciting new market; the second, primarily as people in need.

For either one, the ex-minister as he opens the office door is three things:
- a man in urgent need of a job
- a client
- a "surprise package" of saleable talent.

If he has come to one of the long established, licensed employment agencies (legally, only those who market job seekers can call themselves "agencies"), the procedure is straightforward. Personnel Specialties, in New York City (handling only clergy), does a standard placement job. It appraises one's talents and inclinations, matches these with available openings, places him as quickly as possible, and collects its fee (set by law) according to the usual practice. To varying degrees employment agencies engage in job counsel. But job counseling as such differs in one key point: it does not market clients, on the principle that it is better for them to do this themselves.

Human Resource Developers, for instance, gives tests, helps clients identify their marketable skills congruent with career choices, and coaches them in how to approach employers. "We give them a 'lifetime guarantee,' sticking with them until they find what they want," an official explained.

Job counseling differs, too, from classic employment agencies in that it is a new, booming, largely unpoliced field. It grows in response to the fact that more and more people have not one, but several careers in today's lifetime. Affluence, universally available adult education, and the "make the most of this life" philosophy encourage this trend. However, because it is still undisciplined, job counseling features both the best and the worst of ethics and practices.

In December, 1968, the City of New York held a hearing, on the complaints of hundreds of clients who had paid hefty fees to "counselors" and received very little service, from some of the two hundred firms then in the field. Bernard Haldane, who has counseled many ex-ministers and ministers, recommended at that hearing that these companies be licensed, as are the employment agencies, and that they develop, like them, professional associations and a code of ethics. The hearing adjourned with at least one of the "shyster" outfits promising to "consider" returning fees to those dissatisfied.

Reputable job counseling moves, necessarily, far beyond the find-a-slot-and-fill-it-for-a-fee approach. But the unworldly clergy are easy prey for those few who, as in all walks of life, are out to get as much and give as little as they can.

The social service type of operation has human need as its primary concern. Like most service agencies, it begins with one or two selfless individuals, in begged or borrowed quarters. It is held together, on its crisis-and-miracle upward climb, by a dedicated, poorly paid staff which sometimes skips paydays altogether. Volunteers (largely former clients) stuff envelopes and serve coffee.

Bearings, Inc., and Next Step are of this type. They are always in debt, partly because at most they collect only a fraction of their per-client cost: $35 at Next Step; $100 at Bearings, New York City. Even this is on a pay-later basis. They never have enough rooms or chairs or telephones. More than that, programs keep well ahead of revenue: they put forth branches, spin off subgroups, inspire living communities for clients who have found a new togetherness.

One would think them "naturals" for funding. Actually they are in an awkward position to ask for help. To conventional foundations, they seem too "churchy." But to religious funds and potential donors, they seem threatening, subversive, and suspect of "seducing" clergy.

Clerics Anonymous

Helping clergy take the "next step" or get their "bearings" is much more than the rescue mission their founders had in mind, much more than helping people find a job. Their clients are shaken to the roots of their being. They usually delay leaving until remaining becomes impossible. As one agency director says, "They come to us after the tension is unbearable."

Moreover, they are racked by a *moral* problem. For a great many, it is a positive scandal to leave the pastorate.

Peter Schaeffer, an ex-priest who went to Princeton to work on his doctorate, points out that "Whatever he might say to explain himself (is) only added to his condemnation, as an evidence of his pride." A Catholic layman comments: "No matter what the reason, the public feels these priests have let us and the Church down." Another: "How do I feel about a priest who quits? I guess I feel hostile. I can't see how he can be dispensed from his vows. His vocation is a lifetime commitment."

For the layman, switching from one firm to another, from one kind of work to another is no great thing. Not so for the clergyman. Becoming an "ex" calls into question his total life pattern and his moral integrity.

Hence, breaking with the church is truly like breaking up a marriage. Entry into the occupation is emotionally akin to falling in love. One's commitment to it, solemnized in public ceremony, is like marriage, a sacrament. So the leaving of it goes equally deep.

Leaving not only tears one apart emotionally. In a literal sense it demolishes one as a person, the self adopted in the vows of ordination and confirmed through years of ministry. Ordination, a word derived from *ordo* (order) has both social and ontological references. It connotes entry into a different, special relationship both to God and to one's fellow humans.

In social terms, as an ex-nun says, "You derive your very identity and your worth from the institution. You represent your order, not yourself." This religious institution is part of the total social fabric. And it provides a working relationship with a transcendent realm. To leave breaks not only the clergyman's self-image, but threatens to crack the image other people have of themselves and their world. The defecting pastor affronts everybody's socio-cosmic stability. It is as if he had poked a small hole in the empyrean.

There is, then, something inconceivable about leaving the ministry. For Jew, Protestant, or Catholic, to leave marks the cancellation of a pact with God. There is the element of finality, even death, in it. The ex-clergyman is a strange sort of "ex" with the air of a captain who has deserted his ship, of a suicide who somehow lives to tell his tale.

No wonder no one knows what to say to an ex-pastor! No wonder he throws the workaday world into confusion! No wonder agencies have arisen as bridges to and interpreters of the secular realm.

One ex-priest got a job and went to work. When his status was revealed, they fired him, explaining: "We didn't know you were a 'former.' " It was as if he had "passed," or concealed his having done time in prison. (Indeed, it is no coincidence that one of Next Step's major new projects is a halfway program for ex-convicts.)

Can the ex-pastor really be an ordinary person in a business suit? His new boss and colleagues are used to dealing with the parson at arm's length, as of a different order, not as employee, peer, or pal.

Unless the psychological wrench involved in the break with the church is recognized, no helping program can be adequate. One new help-for-clergy outfit started off its first set of clients discussing the "latest" religious material: Dead Sea Scrolls, Christian origins, etc. The group blew up with a bang: the hell with the Qumran findings: their agenda was themselves and their pent-up agonies!

Directors of agencies on both coasts used the same word to describe some clients: "damaged" persons. A few even have to be hospitalized. "We have to ask ourselves," says the director of the Boston office of Human Resource Developers, "what kind of an operation we have. Is it for normal people, or is it a therapy outfit?" Most offices are for normal people, but there is often a great deal of therapy needed. Some find the best is a kind of "pastors anonymous" which works much as Alcoholics Anonymous or Weight Watchers, i.e. "we're all in this together," or "the fellow who's been there is the best help." Thus, they can ventilate the doubt, the resentment, the uncertainty. They can get rid of their clergyphobia and begin to laugh about "the way those so-and-so's had it in for me."

Finding one is neither alone nor crazy is great medicine. Five priests from the same order had crept away in shock after a traumatic gathering, each not wanting to hurt the others. It chanced they drifted in, one by one, to a clergy-help agency's anteroom next day. Worry changed to astonishment, embarrassment to relief—and finally dissolved in uproarious guffaws, not unmixed with tears of joy.

Whether they intended to or not, conscientious agencies find they must deal with the varied, urgent, and unexpected needs of "formers." To do so, they have mobilized a corps of lawyers, psychiatrists, employment counselors, as well as volunteers to help with housing, hostessing, and personal finance. They have, also, assembled a set of referral buttons to push for persons with special needs. Really distressed ex-clergy can, thus, get "same-day" therapy, as well as extended therapy at special rates. Free blood is available for Next Step's San Francisco clients in emergencies—donated by inmates of San Quentin prison!

Becoming 'People' Again

One of the greatest and most universal needs for these bruised souls is people: people to talk to, people to be with, people who can be just people!

Rabbi, minister, priest, and nun are all, by their ordination, set apart. There are very few to whom they are simple persons, uncomplicated by the role. Once ordained, they become not persons but "pastors" or "fathers" or "rectors" or "rabbis" or "sisters," that is, figures in some way standing over others in judgment or authority or sanctity. They are anything but friends, men, women, peers. James Kavanaugh, the ex-priest psychological counselor, was attracted to his future wife because, when he suggested vaguely that they might date, she said "My name's in the phone book!" As a priest, he had been used to deference. Her tart response was personal, human!

Next Step thus began with and still features evening open houses, just for getting together over coffee and wine with other clergy, ex-clergy, and sympathetic laypersons. Special days and holidays are always covered: Hallowe'en or Valentine's Day or Thanksgiving, the loneliest times for "all the lonely people." A former nun serves as volunteer hostess at Bearings' Tuesday open houses held in the basement of the Episcopal Church of the Resurrection, New York. ("Church of the Insurrection" those who come call it.)

For many, sociability soothes an ache that has been buried under the old notion that defection is something you keep dark. One of Restivo's aims in starting Bearings was to break through such stifling secrecy, exemplified by a little old lady who came to Next Step. She had renounced her vows, privately, in 1921, almost half a century before. Only after all those lonely years was she at last able to say "Now I can come and talk about it and enjoy it all!"

But even sociability isn't to be had just for the asking. In the big city, people who want to meet people are told: go to a discotheque. How can you manage this if you can't dance? So, dancing has been added—folk, ballroom, rock. A Bearings spinoff developed when twenty ex-nuns took a house in New Jersey, to learn to dance, shop, cook, swim, and date. It developed into a living group, a community house. Before long, another was in the works: a ski lodge!

One major aspect of ex-clergy personal adjustment is marriage. Agencies, of course, serve as dating bureaus. Some clients hit the jackpot with a wedding. There are no figures available now, but a notable statistic will be the number of ex-priests who marry ex-nuns. Here is a "natural"—a readiness, a desire to share, a lifetime of pent-up emotional longing, mutual experience and understanding. The emancipated priest and nun who find each other may be a classic romance of our time. Surely Héloise and Abelard must be smiling somewhere.

Bill and Carole Tegeler of Chicago come to mind in this context. Bill is a former Roman, later Eastern Orthodox, priest; Carole, for fourteen years a Franciscan sister. Now they live in a large house called "Camelot," where they are open to "formers." Indeed they have made their home into a halfway house, so organized in March, 1969.

Many an ex-priest or ex-nun is drawn, however, to another sort of "ex": a man or woman with experience of the world including a ready-made family. Here is good news for the widowed or divorced who must cope as parents without partners: typical is the forty-nine-year-old former Dominican nun who married a widower with four children.

But one problem lurks. According to Robert Duggan, the first coordinator of the National Association for Pastoral Renewal (Catholic), often the man is so starved for genuine human response that the "first warm woman to be nice to him, just human, completely throws him. He may flip over her, even though she's actually a nothing. He may wake up later to find, not a marvellous relationship, but the ashes of an immediate urgency."

Patricia Roy, of Bearings, adds that nuns, too, have been in the same state of naïveté. "For ten or twelve years during training, most priests and sisters are taught that friendship is a no-no. Until recently, the perfect nun was one who was totally self-contained. The inability to relate to others is a Pavlovian response: the appearance of warmth is a bell that rings, saying 'Danger! Run the other way!' "

On the Protestant and Jewish side there is the same problem in reverse. Many have had to leave the church because of a marital problem. In some denominations, divorce means out: out altogether, or at least out of sight. There are many who leave in order to divorce, or to divorce and remarry. Many more leave in order to save the marriage; the ministerial situation proves to be "just too much." So, helping agencies, though they didn't expect to, find themselves involved with marriage counseling. Bearings' midwest office, for example, offers a seminar for couples.

Learning to Walk Alone

First Aid for an immediate crisis is often what brings the agencies and the refugees together. They will come direct to the Bearings office, say, off a plane from Mexico or South America—anxious, bewildered, often broke. They need, immediately, little loans for a few nights' lodging, groceries, or bus fare. They may even have to fall back on the Bearings cot in the back office as an overnight crash pad.

And, while they sort things out, they are given temporary jobs: night watchman, hospital orderly, cab driver.

Almost unbelievably, some ex-religious do not know how to manage simple mechanics of everyday living—how to cook a meal or shop for it, what clothes to buy, or how much to pay for them. Especially for priests and nuns, the world outside the cloister is like Mars. Some of them have had everything done for them. They cannot dress their hair or tie a necktie. They have to be told: "Don't pay more than a week's salary for rent or you'll be broke by payday."

Their problem comes from one or the other side of their vow of poverty. For many, poverty has meant "denying themselves" all but bare essentials. Now they must adjust

to the comforts of a commercial society. Sometimes the reaction is extreme. One former nun of twenty-five years'
service was interviewed in a posh beauty salon. She makes
a good salary in social welfare, to which she is devoted. Her
new motto, though, is "nothing but the best." She lives
in fashionable Stuyvesant Village, dines out in restaurants
(checking the gourmet guide for stars), buys her clothes at
Lord and Taylor, enjoys tasteful jewelry and her wiglet.
However, she is anything but frivolous. "I have not broken
with the Church," she says. "I'm earning these things and I
savor them. I feel I am being religious 'outside,' and an ap-
preciation of good taste is a part of being so."

On the other hand, many in the Roman Church, despite their vow of poverty, find that cloistered living, para-
doxically, turns out to be a kind of collective affluence. They
too emerge as babes, because they have had everything done
for them: they have had cooks, housekeepers, maids, chauf-
feurs, secretaries, gardeners. A financially pinched staff member figured that one of her helpless clients, under the vow of
poverty, had the benefit of what a $25,000 annual salary
might buy—but of course without the opportunity to decide
how and for what it should be spent.

Gnawing at the conscience of such cushioned cap-
tives is, that their work, all along, has been with the poor; some,
perhaps, preaching to the poor of the hustling city. No
wonder, then, there are sessions on money and budgets and
insurance; on clothes and make-up and dancing and how to
drive an auto; field trips to supermarkets, and kitchen labs for
cookery. Beyond this, groups develop interests and skills: encounter and creative writing and body awareness, poetry and
play-reading, ski weekends, leatherwork, yoga and guitar.
Not long ago Bearings got this note: "I'm glad to send you, to
say thanks, my first check, from the first checkbook I've ever
had!"

And Incidentally, Jobs

The purpose for which most of these agencies were first set up and the immediate necessity in the minds of their arriving clients, is jobs. Job placement is not the most important problem which some of these people initially face, but it is the peg on which the whole process hangs, the focus and excuse for other things.

Almost all ex-clergy need the ABC's of how to apply for a job: how to draw up a résumé, how to answer the employer's questions (simply, without sermonizing). Even when they become conscious of what a skill is, they generally have little idea which skills can be marketed, to what jobs or careers they apply, or how to market them.

Bearings has a standard four-session program:

Monday: THE JOB MARKET: ". . . a basic description of different careers, various types of jobs . . . what is involved in each."

Tuesday: RÉSUMÉ: an inventory of the client's own skills, interests, aptitudes.

Wednesday: JOB OBJECTIVES: ". . . to produce one or two objectives suitable to the career you wish to pursue . . . translating valuable church experience into marketable terms."

Thursday: JOB INTERVIEW TECHNIQUES AND EVALUATION: ". . . the logistics of the interview . . . how to evaluate (it) and determine your next step."

Evening sessions are both social, and programmed for "how to" topics such as making a personal budget.

A happy surprise has been that ex-clergy have skills they have never thought of as "skills." A diffident nun, for instance, who has helped staff a girl's school may not realize that, in the world's terms, she has had solid experience as an administrator, budget officer, fund-raiser, public relations expert—and as a teacher and counselor to boot.

Thus Margaret (not her real name: she still fears to embarrass her family and order) began, as a sister, to edit the woman's page of the diocesan paper, and wrote a newsletter for her community. After she left, an agency assisted her to market these skills as an editor for a textbook publisher. To-day she helps the agency with its public relations writing.

Clergy have training that translates in unexpected ways. James Lowery of the Boston Human Resource Developers says "We've found that a cleric who is able to handle systematic theology has an almost ideal predisposition for being a top-notch computer programmer."

More important than any of this, however, in finding and holding a job, is a sense of being worth something, and with it, a willingness to stand up and say so. Job-seeking takes "gumption." Here, clergy must overcome an occupational hazard. "Humble yourself" is the scripturally sanctioned attitude, becoming a "servant" of God and man. When one has spent a professional lifetime trying to internalize "humility," reversing it to sell one's worth to an employer comes as something of a sin as well as a shock.

Moreover, the church has not only made a virtue of passivity; it has built it into its system. From the very beginning, most churches stress reactive, rather than pro-active, behavior. It starts with being "called" rather than choosing one's occupation. It is reinforced thereafter at almost every point by the role stereotypes and procedures of the church: Protestant, Catholic, or Jewish. God calls, congregations call, bishops assign, and it is bad ministerial ethics for a pastor actively to seek advancement. Instead, he waits for the bureaucracy to move him. No wonder that stiffening the back-bone, and assuring the client it is a virtue to help himself, are basic in giving ex-clergy a fresh hold on life.

Success?

Do ex-clergy successfully cross the bridge to secular life and work? If "success" means job placement, they certainly are successful. Agencies point to hundreds and hundreds, in teaching and social work, business and industry, government and all manner of self-employment, whose transition they helped make possible.

One Washington agency measures success, quite frankly, in terms of salary bracket. It is very proud of the fact that the average starting salary for clients is $13,000, and that some have begun as high as $36,000.

For others, however, this is not what success means. In the words of Katie Murphy of Chicago's Bearings: "We can quote lots of cases of ex-priests getting $15,000 a year or more, but that's not the success story we're most interested in. It's the man who gains peace and, at whatever level, re-dedicates himself as a Christian." Says another director: "Success is not 'serving,' not even serving humanity. It is becoming a human being."

One "success" who volunteers part-time help to the agency that assisted her, now lives with her parents, dates occasionally, and seems to ask little of life except one thing —the opportunity to continue to grow. "Nothing more than that, but nothing less, either." There is the ex-nun who qualifies as a "success" though she leads a simple, unpretentious life as a librarian. She has picked up the pieces of her life, gotten rid of her hangups, knows who she is. All she asks now is to lead her own life, in quiet comfort and in peace.

The ex-clergy client is at first preoccupied with immediate bread-and-butter questions. His days and nights are filled with hard work: homework, preparing résumés, self-assessment, tests, interviews. After he gets a job the pace slows down. Then the deeper questions press. What is, what should be, his stance with respect to the church? *Now* is he for it, against it, with it, out of it? What gestures should he make?

Sometimes he returns to the parish ministry. The break was what he needed, to give him new perspective, new commitment. But most likely he will not return. How shall he think about himself and his career in the long run? In leaving the church, has he left the ministry? What does "ministry" mean now? Who is he, if he is no longer defined by the religious institution?

As a worker with many such clients observed: "When the former shepherd finds himself one of the flock, his view may be somewhat different. Someone who was sure he liked working with people now finds this isn't true. He's actually more comfortable with ideas or commodities."

The agency, too, if it is anything more than a straight job placement outfit, has to ask itself the big questions: what is *it* about? After applying the bandaids, what are its long range goals? What is its fundamental position on the ministry, per se, and the church?

Some agencies save people *for* the church, some *from* it, some *for themselves*. John Mulholland of the Program Planning Institute, takes a straight business approach. "It's no different with clergy," he says, "than with anyone else changing careers. There's nothing wrong with these people that a good job can't fix."

The Santa Barbara organization, Professional Refocus Operation, "for church alumni and those on the inside edge" modeled after the approach of the late James Pike who originated it, says "The church is finished. Get out and become 'church alumni' and in this, we will help you."

The national director of Bearings says "We meet the

person where he is, with no foregone plans or conclusions
. . . We don't ask why they leave but why they entered.
This tells us about them, and gives us a clue as to what we
should do."

Many entered as children. Tom Lynch, a former
missionary priest, now an estates estimator at Chemical Bank
in New York, says: "I was seventeen and trying to get away
from parental control. I suppose I was partly interested in
becoming a priest, but mostly looking for an escape. It just
seemed to offer a worthwhile life and a means of finding myself. I don't think I really thought deeply about the state I
was entering."

A nun who made the decision to enter the church at
the age of eighteen says, "Religiously I was a child. I think
that eighteen is a very young age to enter into a permanent
commitment. . . . I didn't have a total picture of myself,
nor what my actual life and circumstance would be. Gradually I found my interests becoming different from what my
kind of life would allow me to pursue. Academically and
socially I had broadened considerably but my opportunities
had not."

"Later," she said thoughtfully, "we are going to have
to re-think a lot of things. We seem to be in an age right
now, when many people are questioning the feasibility of
any kind of a permanent contract."

In the 1966–1968 study of diocesan priests, Joseph
Fichter reports (*America's Forgotten Priests: What They
Are Saying*) that the average age of entering the priesthood
is seventeen. Twenty-seven percent of his respondents entered at thirteen and fourteen, ten percent at fifteen and six-
teen. "If they could do it over again, the general tendency is
to avoid such an early entrance to the seminary."

These cases are not exceptional; certainly not just
Catholic.

Little wonder, then, that in dealing with the ex-pastor, questions of identity, self-direction, and maturity assume major importance. Leaving the church may have represented not failure or regression, but growth. As a thirty-four-year-old teaching brother confessed: "The only real decision I've ever made is to leave. Even deciding to enter the order was a joint decision, not mine."

Along with their clients, the agencies grow in their self-image and philosophy. Says Patricia Roy: "We want to get people out of their own ghetto. We want this to be a place where the person, the whole person, can find out who he is and what he can do. Our long range goals are to make easier the long range goals of these people."

Where Is It All Going?

What the field will look like, and where it will be even six months from now is hard to say. In six months what has been described here may be unrecognizable in "a brand new ball game."

What began as a rescue mission outside, may become an arm of the larger church system. Agencies which were seen at the start as "subversive," interpreted as enticing and seducing the clergy away, are becoming now a part of the broader church. They are increasingly consulted by secretaries and bishops and departments of ministry. They are being used by church executives for referral of distressed and problem personnel. They are being called in at conferences and symposia to register their views, and are being used officially as consultants.

Bearings is represented, for example, on the church-operated Career Development Council. This is consistent with its director's statements, that with competent career counseling at the right moment, many clergy would not need to leave. "We wish the churches would assume this task," says she.

All of them—pastors, ex-pastors, agencies, and churches, are having to push further and further back for solutions to their problems. Where does a solution begin? Certainly, not with leaving the church.

Should these ex-clergy have become clergy in the first place? What about the church selection procedures? What about the seminary: was preparation realistic and adequate? What about the years after seminary, out in the field? Were there places for retooling and updating? Places to go with questions? People to talk with when they were troubled about church problems, career, marriage?

For an increasing number of knowledgeable people in and connected with churches, the answer is unanimous. In all of these stages much more is called for: a whole new philosophy of problem prevention and aid, far back and all along the way; a fresh approach to the profession of ministry in positive, developmental terms, as a career which needs continuous tending, refreshment, and nurture.*

In the meantime, at least some of these centers, ferreting out and serving the needs of those who come to them, and playing totally by ear, *themselves* have become, for these troubled people, *a new kind of church*.

* See below, Chapters VIII and IX, and bibliography for fuller discussion.

second oldest profession

The ministry is in trouble. Worse, it is confused. In this, there is considerable irony. From time immemorial, the man of religion has held the surest, most respected place, whether as shaman of a primitive tribe, church scholar of the Middle Ages, or parson—*the* learned man—of a New England village. For decades, his hold on the number one spot in America's prestige careers was firm. Theology, described by Auguste Comte as the crown and apex of the scientific hierarchy, was for centuries the "queen of sciences."

Stranger still, the greatest confusion is found among clergy themselves. What other profession calls meetings to ask itself what it should be doing? Who else resists the label "profession"? Outside their ranks, it is taken for granted that ministry is a profession. It is listed as such in occupation studies, social science texts, and the United States Census. Yet to pastors, more often than not, the word is anathema. The Rev. Bryan Kirkland of the Fifth Avenue Presbyterian Church of New York City, for example, told a gathering of 700 United Methodist ministers in January, 1969, at all costs to avoid the "danger of professionalism." Thus, uncounted numbers of workers in dozens of occupations covet the label; stenographers, beauty operators, and undertakers "profession-alize" themselves into secretaries, cosmetologists, and morti-cians; while bona fide professionals in the field of religion avoid the term like the plague.

This anomaly was pointed up not long ago in a book by James Glasse, *Profession: Minister*, the main point of which was to sell the profession to clergy themselves!

Different Drummers

What is it about "profession" that drives clergy up the wall? To begin with, it has all the wrong connotations. It smacks of fees and performance and standards and contracts —which is not where the pastor lives. He experiences and understands his work as a "calling," the term he uses most generally and naturally and with which he feels most com-fortable.

The clash between "profession" and "calling" is more than a matter of word choice, however, and more than semantics. The two represent nothing less than contrasting philosophies and approaches to a career. As Glasse observed, the critical issue is not the clergyman's ecclesiastical identity in the church, but his occupational identity in the world of work.

In the eyes of its practitioners, the work of ministry is by nature and by definition inherently one of a kind. To the social analyst, it is part of an occupational category, that is, but one of a class. This difference in perspective has driven a wedge between sociologists and clergy. To ministers, such categorization hints of sacrilege, and appears to challenge ministerial uniqueness. Understandably, there are few studies by clerics on the pastorate as a profession. For social scien-tists, on the other hand, in an age increasingly profession-minded, separation of ministry from occupational categories renders it even more dated, irrelevant and out of touch.

Some key contrasts between "profession" and "calling":

First, at the point of entry, one chooses a profession on the basis of cool and calculated decision. Service to man is part of the motivation, of course, but one expects adequate compensation for his service, and a good living.

Even today, however, the pastor takes up his work not as a careful career choice, but as something he must do. In the tradition of a Moses, Paul, or Gautama, he is somehow grasped in spite of his "kicking against the pricks." He does not choose to be a pastor, he is chosen. For most clergymen, this calling is an irresistible summons from a higher plane.

The professional model goes back to humanist Greece, and has to do with the everyday world. The traditional, and still fundamental reference for most pastors, however, is to a Kingdom not of this world, but transcending and judging it by nonworldly, that is, nonmonetary standards.

The professional sees himself as a master of his field and of his skills. Clergy try to avoid such power-laden, "arrogant" concepts. The parson thinks of himself not as master, but as servant: servant of the Lord, servant of the church, servant of mankind.

While professionals evaluate themselves and their performance in terms of salary and promotion, clergy do not. They often identify with such humble referents as the "suffering servant," measuring or rationalizing their "success" by inverse or nonmundane standards. (Why else would clergy across the denominational spectrum be willing to accept substandard incomes?)

And finally, to cite yet another contrast in terms of rewards, the two are accorded different kinds of social status. Professional status is achieved. Ministerial status, as sociologists would have it, is ascribed. In a profession, no one is taken for granted. He must qualify to enter, train to perform, deliver to succeed, and, throughout his career, continue to deliver. The ministry as a calling, is understood as having inherent value, independent of achievement. In every society, some element of divinity has been counted as essential, and has been symbolized therein with something of the once-removed aura of royalty. A king is a king is a king, quite apart from appearance, ability, intelligence, training. So with the representative of religion.

To be sure, society has domesticated divinity, institutionalized it, and created a vehicle for the one "called." It has "routinized charisma" as Max Weber described it. To be sure, if the parson is blessed with a golden voice, a great vision, an irresistible presence; if, like St. Ambrose, he has the business genius which the religious institution needs, then he will "make it" in worldly terms as well.

But these are extras. One can be a "success" as a clergyman even if he is a "failure" in worldly terms. Indeed, the pastor's proverbial ineptness and gullibility are taken as a sort of "proof" of spirituality. What matters is that the man of God serve as a reminder of the presence of God in this world.

Clearly, notions as disparate and contrasting as these of spiritual calling and worldly profession are bound to be fraught with tension. But how, if such profound differences between them exist, has it been possible to classify ministry as a profession?

For all its differences, it does share with many occupations such characteristics as: a special and historic body of knowledge, requisite skills, serious commitment, personal responsibility and accountability, in work for the service of man. With others, it requires a substantial period of preparation, a relevant institution, and a related clientele.

Justice Brandeis summed up profession as

An occupation for which the necessary preliminary
training is intellectual in character, involving
knowledge, and, to some extent, learning, rather
than mere skill; which is pursued largely for others
and not merely for oneself, and in which financial
return is not the accepted measure of success.

For all its devotion to the good of mankind, ministry
can hardly be thought of as the only career "pursued largely
for others and not merely for oneself." Nor does ministry
have a monopoly on the principle that "financial return is
not the accepted measure of success." Nursing and teaching
and social work all come to mind.

Both sides in this running but unarticulated controversy are correct. The ministry is a profession among other
professions. It is also a profession with a difference.

Part of the clergyman's problem is that, in practice,
he has not been able to hold on to "calling" in its pure and
undiluted form. Unconsciously, he has accepted and ab-
sorbed many of the standards and principles of professionalism which surround him, while retaining the fundamental
loyalty to the idea of calling. The Rev. Mr. Kirkland sensed
the problem: when one begins to judge a calling by professional standards, trouble begins.

As with any profession, two key areas of ministry are
its esoteric body of knowledge, and its particular clientele.
Both are pressing problem areas today. In each, the traditional
concept of ministry and the traditional concept of profession clash sharply.

Professionals Without Portfolio

That special "body of knowledge," the intellectual
component to which Brandeis referred, has long been a

stumbling block for clergy. At the very outset, the question arises: Can a spiritual calling be taught? Many in the Western church have for centuries contended that it cannot.

The early Quakers were among those whose fear of learning and "the ways of learned men" led them to feel that they "needed no man to teach them but the Lord was their teacher." In 1652, Society of Friends founder George Fox wrote in his journal: "As I was walking in a field on a first-day morning, the Lord opened unto me, 'That being bred at Oxford or Cambridge was not enough to fit and qualify men to be ministers of Christ.'"

And how many have held Tyndale's conviction that "the boy following the plough could know his Bible as well as the gravest doctor" and that "clergie men are in no more relation to God than other men"? For these, education is, rather, the enemy of religious fervor. A large proportion, perhaps a majority, of American preachers today feel no need of seminary.

If one accepts the principle of education for ministry, however—and concern for a "learned ministry" led to the founding of Harvard College in 1636—another problem lies in wait at the seminary door. How should the student applicant be received? Should there be standards of excellence and screening for prospective clergy? Can a person who is "called" be refused? As for the seminary itself: what is the clergyman's subject matter and area of expertise? A body of knowledge? Or a set of techniques?

Prior to the present "crisis of faith" (discussed in Chapter II), this question had an accepted, and acceptable, answer. The clergyman studied the "body of divinity," that is, the Scriptures, and the vast and majestic theological superstructure erected thereon by the labors of the Church's thinkers down the ages. The goal of those labors was to arrange all human experience into a framework of understanding vouchsafed by Revelation.

Clergy have always chosen this body of knowledge, and shunned "mere technical aspects" of the religious institution. To this day, studies such as theology, Biblical exegesis, church history, and their professorships, rate much higher in seminaries than do the "practical" disciplines, including such fashionable ones as pastoral counseling.

Now, however, this body of divinity has been eroded by the "acids of modernity." Truth is no longer apprehended by revelation, and many vast philosophical structures are no longer acceptable.

The lawyer's esoteric body of knowledge—the law; the dentist's—his sector of medicine; the engineer's—mechanics; the triumph of science has enlarged to the point of surfeit. But the victory of the empirical and humanistic has disintegrated the minister's special province—the "body of divinity"—leaving him a professional without portfolio.

To be sure, he is left with one legacy from the past: he is still a dealer in meaning, concerned literally with everything. But today, so is everybody else! Is anyone's opinion on "meaning" more valuable than any other's? What now sets the minister apart from a professor of ethics, a social critic, or a well-rounded newspaper columnist, for that matter, so far as he is a witness to values in events?

A Curious Clientele

If the minister's relation to a professional body of knowledge poses a problem, so does his clientele.

The doctor is employed by an individual with whom he has a very direct and immediate relationship. The lawyer or architect is hired by a person or a firm; the administrator or engineer by an institution. Each of them is engaged for a specific assignment or purpose.

Not so the minister. His clientele is both an individual person and a congregation—a congregation which changes from month to month, whose members come and go, in response, partly, to satisfactions they derive from his work.

The minister has no clear contract with his clients as do other professionals. He is not hired for a definite time to do a definite job, but for an indefinite period for an uncertain array of activities. His work is difficult to delineate in precise terms. At the same time, it is so public and visible that all his parishioners have a firm opinion of him and his job. Since the goals are seldom sharply enough defined for objective evaluation, the pastor is evaluated nontechnically in fuzzy, cumulative, and conflicting subjective reactions by his "sidewalk superintendents." Unlike a doctor or lawyer, whose clients contract to follow his prescriptions or counsel, the minister's clients can take it or leave it. Moreover, they sit in judgment on him!

It is commonplace for people to leave a church on whim or when a pet idea is stepped on: "That last sermon *did* it!" As Rabbi Herbert Tarr has noted—a clergyman is the only professional whose clients can gang up at the end of the year and cancel him. And as Tarr's rabbi in *Heaven Help Us* moans:

> All year long now I've preached essentially one sermon: that religion is a demand and God the challenger . . . Yet how many got the message, when no requirements whatsoever are demanded of congregants? And so religion inevitably ends up the name people give their own biases.

Like the old country doctor, the pastor is always "on call" for consultations, emergencies, deaths. Unlike the doctor, he has no retreat or fortress to which he can escape. In most cases, his "castle" is the property of his client. (Says one observer: "He is a 'kept' man.") Not only does he work in the limelight, he must answer in his off hours as well, for his life in the parsonage.

Beyond his congregation, he has a boss once removed. Unlike most individuals or firms of professionals, he works also under the eye of his denomination. The degree of pressure he feels here varies from church to church, but in almost all of them it becomes acute in terms of his professional advancement.

Almost universally the kind of denominational pressure is depressingly institution-oriented. To stand in well with Headquarters, he needs to be loyal to the system. The obverse side of this pressure is lack of official support, for him as a person, in anything that departs too far from usual and accepted ways of operating.

The clergyman can't change the nature of his clientele. But his relationship with them can be improved. Much of what is called for depends on his own change from the traditional clerical mind-set that thinks only of duties and not of corresponding rights.

One hears increasingly of a brash and determined pastor here and there who draws up for his future congregation a bill of particulars on where he stands, how he works, what he does best, what he will or will not do. Boards seem to be relieved to have such a clear-cut contract, and even more relieved to have a parson with backbone and some business sense. Even in churches, "Good fences make good neighbors." Gradually, clergy are learning this. Even in their professional associations, they have begun to make union-like noises and moves.

One argument for a married clergy may be that the minister's wife often contributes an element of earthy reality to his dealings with the deacons. She cannot afford to have his lofty distaste for definite business arrangements. It is not that she is unspiritual or unsympathetic. But she was not "called," and she has to think of clothes for the kids and repairs for the washing machine. A rector's wife reminisced: "When we went to a church in New England, many years ago, my husband expansively explained to the selection committee: 'Don't worry a bit about salary. The matter of money is irrelevant to me.' " "Well," she said, "it wasn't to *me!*"

It may be that a minister's relation to his parish is most like a marriage. (As his wife perceives it, a *rival* marriage.) And as in any marriage, the basic sentiment of love has to be translated into mutually clear and understood working relationships. In any case, it is a day-in, day-out, no-escape affair, and when anything goes wrong, there is sadness and regret and pain on both sides.

Revelation: Sociological

Clergy and sociologists have gone separate ways—with one outstanding exception: when the sociologist began to analyze the minister's job. Here what he found spoke aptly to the troubled parson who welcomed it.

It is not too much to say that, until they were subjected to this sort of scrutiny, clergy literally did not know what they were doing. Their doctrinal, deductive thought-categories, productive of lofty rationalizations rather than critical description, were simply inappropriate to functional analysis.

The findings of the social scientists came with all the force of a new "revelation" to pastors, who had been working more and enjoying it less, but could not quite say why. These analysts convinced them, that whatever one may say about the ministry as a "calling," as an occupation it is enough to try the patience of a saint.

The studies focused on the work of the parish ministry, with which ministry is usually equated. Research zeroed in particularly on a breakdown of the minister's roles. Some studies named six, some eight, some twelve. A typical listing went like this:

- preaching
- teaching
- counseling (including parish calling and spiritual first aid)
- administration
- organization and fundraising
- priestly functions: weddings, funerals, Bar Mitzvahs, Eucharist, cornerstone blessings
- leader, spokesman, symbolic representative of religion in the community.

This inventory, with appropriate variations, applied to Methodist preacher, Roman Catholic parish priest, or Reform rabbi. As it turns out, today, they all wind up doing much the same thing.

Such studies brought harsh new light, but no help or relief, to the man of the cloth. One look at the number and range of tasks expected of him was enough to drive all but the strongest to a state of despair. How could he possibly be an expert, or even passably good, in so many fields and in such varied specialities?

The *coup de grâce* was delivered by Samuel Blizzard's blockbuster study of 690 sample clergymen, released in popular form as an article called "The Minister's Dilemma" (*Christian Century*, April, 1956).

The "minister's dilemma" is that he spends most of his time doing what he least enjoys. He likes best being pastor and preacher. He spends most of his time and energy on organization and administration. Even worse, perhaps, these are precisely the areas in which he is least prepared: seminaries skip or downgrade such fields as human relations and organizational management.

Later research sharpened his discomfort. In a survey of how parishioners feel about their minister's work, it turned out that laymen also dislike the preoccupation with nontraditional activities. They would like more time spent on preaching and priestly functions.

All this is a shattering blow to the minister's self-image of his lofty "calling." He may have felt called to help save his fellow men and the world, but the social scientists revealed him to himself as, in practice, an *ecclesiastical organization man*. Sometimes, even worse: a custodian!

Because it offered a handle to the minister's dilemma, clergy quickly accepted this new way of viewing the ministry in terms of roles. It offered them a potential solution, namely, to determine which role, or roles, had priority. It offered, also, a pat diagnosis for why ministers are cracking up—the forerunner to the problem of the 1970's: why ministers are quitting.

A major legacy of the role-analysis approach is the understanding of the parish career as that of a generalist. "Generalist" because the minister performs a complex of diverse and disparate roles. But for him, it has been out of the frying pan, into the fire. Other than that of "calling," few notions have so blocked and confused the minister's professional self-understanding as has the now-accepted role concept of "generalist."

Precinct Captain

True, the parish minister works in many capacities and contexts. But he is a *specialist*. Among other things, and central to them, he directs a voluntary association called a congregation. He is responsible for coordinating its many parts, people, activities, and programs. His specialty is knowing (sensing) where people are, finding out where they want to go, artfully contributing his own insights, and helping them get there.

In the effort to identify and analyze "success" in the parish ministry, one denomination studied eight clergymen, rated successful by peers, congregations and staff members. When the findings were in, officials declared that parish success remained as mysterious and uncertain as ever. The ministers varied greatly in origin, education, and type of church served. Their styles were individual and altogether different from one another. In short, the report declared, they had nothing in common, except that they were "on top of their job" and "able to assess objectively the current condition of their group . . . in an indirect way seeing to it that good end results were being achieved."

Translation: "All eight were good politicians."

Every minister is a people-helper, but whatever else he may be, the parish minister must also be a politician in the dictionary sense: "One versed in the science and art of government."

The minister's relationship to his people is in many ways more like that of a politician to his constituency than that of a professional to his clients. Typically, he builds up an increment of supporters and dissidents. There may come a crisis, from inside or out, which centers on him as a person. He may win a vote of confidence, or be voted out of office, in which case he moves on to repeat the process elsewhere.

Few careers are predicated on such a shifting and transitory principle; few require such a sequence of uprooting and fresh starts. In fact, the latter feature puts a premium on the parson's political skills. At the same time, having to be a model of puritan rectitude is a handicap that does *not* burden the secular politico!

Here again, the parson's situation can be improved,

immediately and in several ways. To begin with, the true nature of parish work can be recognized. As one church management consultant has suggested: "The parish *is* politics! Let's admit it and train for it."

If this is shocking, it is also plain to see that clergy fall into two camps: those who enjoy "helping people relate and make their own decisions," and those who complain that "having a hundred bosses drives me crazy" and despair, as one of these latter put it, "of an institution with as imprecise a goal and commitment as an umbrella."

The two camps have the same religious concern for the whole person, the same ethical fervor. Both views are valid. Each is appropriate for the person involved. But they have conflicting views of personal ministry. Those who enjoy *people* and *process* and *politics*, who are adept at keeping the show on the road and moving it along, are more "successful" in the specialty of presiding over a parish.

Others, more task-, or product-oriented, or with single-track minds and the impatient urge to follow a particular channel—social action, theological scholarship, sensitivity training—are ministers, yes, but more suited to other kinds of ministerial specialty: teaching, counseling, campus ministries, for example.

In the long run, the parish actually functions as a sort of screen, screening *in* those with political aptitude, screening *out* those who lack it. The woods are full of this second type who have, sooner or later, made their way out, or have been helped out, of the parish.

It is unfortunate that the nature of parish work and the difference in ministerial inclinations and talents have not been clearly recognized. If denominations accepted such facts of religious institutional life, they could select for, educate, and provide support for, the various ministerial specialties, including the parish.

This would not deny ministry or calling, but would

capitalize on the scriptural "diversity of gifts" by which the calling is made effective. It would also help break the stranglehold of a number of accepted but unworkable notions: e.g. of parish as *the* ministry, the *only* ministry; of single-track seminary training for one type of clergy—scholar-preachers; of the assumption that parish skills will take care of themselves.

Today, seminaries are crowded with people neither desirous of, nor suited to, parochial work. The parishes are full of the same kind of misfits. The problem is now being solved case by case, in a series of harrowing personal ordeals which culminate in the exodus of bruised souls who are not "making it" in the parish. They are labelled "failures" by the defensive institution, while, with no help from the churches which ordained them, they grope after a new life or truer ministries elsewhere.

The Stone That Was Rejected

In theory, and in practice, clergy have looked down on the "practical skills." However, if one accepts the reality —even more, the opportunity—of the parish ministry, then this "stone that was rejected" may turn out to be the "head of the corner." For, while clergy have rejected such expertise, the times, and the laity, have not: business, government, and other professions reach out to the growing field of interpersonal relations and organizational development as a key to personal and institutional effectiveness.

Moreover, as individual clergymen are discovering, the techniques of applied behavioral science are transforming parishioners' lives more dramatically than preaching at them ever did! These skills may even provide the "how" for the traditional "what" of the church, that is, the down-to-earth means for fulfilling its idealistic message of love.

"Community" is the deep need and special province

of the church. Mastery of the means of obtaining it is the province of the minister.

A New Theology

It is not coincidental that the body of esoteric knowledge—"divinity"—has disintegrated at the very moment that the science of interpersonal techniques is taking shape. This is one of the areas of exploding knowledge out of which a new theology is a-borning. Explicit in the new field are working assumptions about human potential, and a lively and functional "faith."

One of the prophets of this coming theology was the bold theoretician of humanistic psychology, Abraham Maslow, who, at the time of his death in 1970, was engaged in a four-year reflection on the perennial religious issue, the problem of evil. Earlier, his case studies had, in effect, brought William James' classic *Varieties of Religious Experience* into twentieth—even twenty-first—century context.

Contradicting the old, the new theology boldly asserts that people have worth, are not "miserable sinners"; that they have a potential scarcely tapped or dreamed of. This potential can be released by encouraging men and women to affirm themselves, instead of trying to suppress the "natural" man beneath a mentally unhealthy "moral man."

This faith is proving itself as good news to growing thousands. It rests on a gathering body of evidence and experience, mastery of which will call for as much scholarship, plus much more clinical experience, as the old prowess in the domain of theology ever called for.

Profession with a Calling

The fear of "professionalizing" the ministry is grounded in the assumption that such a process would wipe out its unique qualities. Clergy can, as a matter of fact, have the best of both worlds: the distinctions and rewards of "calling," the rights-with-responsibilities of profession. The unique traits of ministry do not have to be lost.

It is, after all, the only profession based on *total concern:* the only profession dedicated to the overall well-being of its people, not just to their education, living space, legal protection, physical health, or teeth. Whatever the performance gaps of its instrument, the church, it is the only voluntary association which is explicitly open to, rather than limited by, such divisions as age, race, occupation, sex, and class.

Unique also is the relation of practitioner to profession. In no other work does his "personal witness"—to borrow a term from the religious past—*as such* play such a part. One would not choose or condone a dentist who is a scoundrel, but individual dentists or architects or engineers do not characterize their professions in the same way and to the same extent that men of the cloth are representative of the ministry.

In a peculiar sense, the pastor *is* his, and his people's, religion. For this reason, the traditional self-effacing clerical stance is inappropriate to his aims and theirs, and his milquetoast "servanthood" is singularly ineffective.

He must come face to face with the question of who he is and what is worth giving his life to. He must first save himself. He knows, in his being, in some half-buried way, that until he is a person (in every sense of the word) there will be little of value in his ministry for anyone else.

In earlier days, he could give himself wholly to the "call" through the church, denying himself, forgetting himself in the commitment of a total devotion. How he divided up the roles was almost irrelevant. It was "all for the glory of God" and his own sense of worth was fulfilled. But today, such a sacrificial giving of self speaks not of strength, but of weakness. Here, a page from the professional's book, with its awareness of self, its insistence on conditions and limits and rights, is in order. It may even help to save him.

Whatever his improved rewards in the new dispensation may be—better hours, better pension, better salary—the main rewards of the clergyman will always be intangible and essentially unlistable: the miracle of a ready-made community as he moves into the new town; the warmth and glow of a people's all-seasons' recognition; the surging sense of creativity as he maps out his work; that super-special feeling when the service goes well.

There are the memories of people he *knows* he has helped: the bereaved young couple, the frightened, questing veteran, the lonely widow. There are the doors all over town —not just his own people's doors—that open instantly when he says, "This is Parson Brown."

The Ultimate Dilemma

The parson may worry Blizzard's "dilemma" to death, as he has now continually for a decade and a half: which role *is* most important, preacher or counselor? pastor or organizer? Which should be given priority: in seminary? in parish?

But a far more troublesome dilemma centers in a role Blizzard did not even mention, a role hallowed through history and memorialized in the fiery eye and biting tongue of an Amos or Jeremiah: the role of the prophet which makes the western religious tradition unique.

This is the role that claws at the preacher today, that conflicts with and challenges all the others. Most of his tasks are protective, solicitous, integrative, and binding: as pastor, to comfort and soothe and heal; as priest, to draw the community close in warmth of familiar routine and ritual; as administrator-politician, to nurse and shore up the church institution and watch over its welfare.

His people *do* need comfort. They do need help in binding themselves into a community. His temple does need strengthening.

But he knows the lacks and weaknesses of this temple. He knows its failure to deliver on other needs. He knows that many stones of the temple must be overturned, that the smooth surfaces of his people's ways must sometimes be broken.

So within him, a tempest rages—between the knowledge of things as they are and things as they ought to be. At every point, and in every role, he must decide which way to go.

"To comfort or to challenge?" He is caught between the institution and the urgent winds of change, which blow and swirl and threaten.

An insoluble dilemma? The perceptive minister, making pastoral/professional use of behavioral science, may have one key to its resolution on his parish doorstep. People's frustrated yearning for genuine community, helpless sense of impotence, frightened inability to take hold of their own destiny—all these call for self-insight, getting in touch with themselves, learning how to relate to and work with others.

The minister who takes his political-parish-catalytic role seriously may be able to answer the prophetic call, even here, making of his congregation a laboratory of competence in self-awareness, relatedness, and decision-making.

Except in community one cannot become a person. The individual and the caring community are the world in microcosm. In this manageable-size circle the pastor may help his people fashion a handle for the larger life that has grown uncaring, unwieldy and unresponsive.

His "call" to put things to rights will always be

there. And since prophecy, by definition, sets all human schemes awry, there has never been a formula for handling it. Its solution is intimately and ultimately personal and situational—an intricate balance of choice and insight, commitment and judgment.

One can only say that, far from deciding how many hours to devote to the sermon or how many committee meetings to attend, the major task of the man called to minister is to translate the inevitable tension within himself and his work into his own *modus operandi*, whereby he can, in all he does, in conscience remain spokesman and integrator, prophet and priest.

CHAPTER FIVE

The Other Revolution
-Women-

Those puzzling over the question, What's happening to ministers and the church? forget the timeless adage: "*Cherchez la femme.*" Part of what's happening—a big part—is women. Not only is this a crucial piece in the whole church mosaic, but it is a key to a good many others.

Pandora's Box

The opening. A great many observers see Pope John's Second Vatican Council as the opening of a monumental Pandora's box. There are two versions to this ancient Greek myth: one says that when the box was opened, all the vices and sins, diseases and troubles in the world at once flew out. The other, that all human blessings and joys escaped forever, save only hope.

The conflicting alternatives are most apt in the present instance. Whether the forces unleashed by Vatican II are black demons or bright hopes depends on one's point of view.

However one sees it, part of this unleashing—perhaps

one should say "uncorseting"—is a freshly emancipating concept and context for women in the church. There are historic precedents, to be sure, not remembered by this generation, when women struggled to get out from under the ecclesiastical thumb. But this time is different, for history and the times now conspire to grant them their wish. One whiff of this heady new air, one stretching of wings in the bright open spaces, and it is certain these emancipated vestals will never return.

Even the Vatican's historic "opening" was a strangely ironical event. It was never intended to let these imprisoned females out of their box. However, as Sally Cunneen, an editor of the sophisticated Catholic quarterly *Cross Currents* observes, "Updating a church with millennial roots can have unforeseen consequences."

The plan had been to invite non-Roman observers to attend as honored guests. When Protestant women, in response, appeared at the sessions on the floor of St. Peter's, the incredible fact was out in the open for all to see: though the state of their own orders was up for discussion on the agenda, and they outnumbered men several times over in their organizations, not one Catholic woman was present, or had even been invited! The protest which arose, and then gradually built up, first from one sector, then another, inside and outside the Council chambers, was enough to push the lid up.

But only a crack. One year and four months later, on September 8, 1964, it was reported that women would be permitted to attend *some* sessions of the Ecumenical Council. Certain nuns and leaders of Catholic women's organizations would be admitted as *auditors* of debates of the third session of the Council, on matters of interest to them.

As Editor Cunneen noted: "They could come in

token numbers to the last two sessions to listen: they could not speak from the floor."

Never mind that the debate brought to light an incredible, and for the most part, forgotten backlog of rules and traditions which exclude women from participation—to say nothing of leadership—or treat them as minors. At the Third World Congress of the Lay Apostolate in Rome, in October, 1967, all the canon laws subjecting Catholic women to inferior positions were still in effect. The lid had been pried open, and it was now just a matter of time.

The message is clear. Mrs. Cunneen's major interest was in what came out of the box. This she explored in some detail in a questionnaire sent to subscribers of her magazine. Though her 1576 respondents were varied, most of them were well-educated Catholics. Concentrating on the women, in 1968 she reported her findings in a book: *Sex: Female; Religion: Catholic.* These women's comments and attitudes are applicable to non-Catholics, to the current scene generally.

Canon Law 813 may still deny women the right to serve Mass, and 1327 may forbid their preaching in the absence of clergy, but the message is clear:

- Women have come out of the box and have no intention of climbing back in.
- They are asserting themselves as never before.
- They have bought the "personhood gospel" and intend to preach and *practice it* full force.

Some verbatim responses about women and the church, in reply to the Cunneen inquiry:

- I don't think the church should have any 'concept of woman' at all. Part of the problem is that they did have one, which had no basis in reality. They should forget the whole thing and let us be ourselves.

- Just for the record, I don't want to be a priest, but damn it, I want to make that choice myself and not have it made for me.
- [Women] know they have the intellectual ability to offer more to the Church, but feel guilty if they try to use it.
- I desire the abolition of sexual discrimination just as I desire the abolition of racial discrimination. Both are equally unjust and irrational.
- The Church does not recognize women as persons, but still classifies them with minors and slaves. She thinks of woman as childbearer, laundress, cook, or nun hiding in a cloister.

What's happening here is happening everywhere, of course, in universities, public forums, on the streets. On March 23, 1970, the San Francisco *Chronicle* reported that "Feminists Are No Joke":

The largest organized feminist group in the country agreed here yesterday that the movement to liberate American women has finally achieved such widespread support that it is no longer being treated as a joke but as a serious revolution.

250 women, ranging from miniskirted career girls to grandmothers in slacks, came together from all parts of the country to attend a three-day conference of the National Organization for Women.

They represented thousands of women in 35 cities who belong to NOW, but they reflect also the views of thousands of other women in the rapidly-growing women's liberation movement. At their meetings, the members of NOW reviewed what was called by one leader 'the mind-boggling successes they have had in their three years of existence.'

They drew up an ambitious program for the future. This included an intensified crusade for the passage of an equal-opportunity amendment to the Constitution.

Mother Church—Father Image

The women's gospel invading the sacred precincts of the church packs a special punch: "Mother Church" has always been male dominated. In the words of one swinging nun, "It's the stag party supreme!"

On closer look, there's something strange about Mother Church. In terms of its organization, development and power, the plot-line is strictly male. Except for Joan of Arc's rude interruption, history treats of it in masculine terms: bony ascetics, bishops in armor, thunderous debates, crusades, inquisitors, and theologians: Ambroses, Gregorys, Jeromes, Chrysostoms, and Xaviers, Luthers and Cromwells, Wesleys, Huses and Mathers. Prophets, popes, and priests are male. It is commonly accepted, now documented by research, that men are much more likely than women to hold top positions in all branches of church leadership.

But the church itself—in its practice and its make-up, its patrons, its devotees—is *overwhelmingly female*. On this, at least, church surveys agree: more women join; more women attend; more women participate. They show more interest than men in religion generally, and perform its rituals more conscientiously, both inside the church and out.

"It is obvious," says Michael Argyle, in his summary of British and American studies, *Religious Behavior*, "that women are more religious on every criterion."

The absurdity of excluding females, traditionally, as well as in the sessions of the Council in Rome, was underlined by Cardinal Leo Joseph Suenens of Malines–Brussels: "Unless I am mistaken, women make up one-half of the world's population." Not so in the church, where they outnumber males by a considerable margin.

One cannot help wondering how woman's numerical and participational predominance, combined with her new-found assertiveness, will affect the destinies of the church.

Pandora's Bag

One immediate outcome, of course, is the new breed of nun who has stamped her little black foot and refused to put up with the same old treatment. Not all, by any means, support change, and some are more than a little shocked by the new goings-on.

A teaching nun in Nova Scotia remarked:

Traditions which are cherished for their familiarity, rather than their effectiveness in our apostolic needs, are not readily distinguished and supplanted by more effective means. Growth is always slow if it is deep. If changes were accepted too readily, they would be suspect because perhaps too superficially adopted.

"Our spiritual training," another volunteered, "offers the individual person a scope of maturation which it would be difficult to improve." From a convent in Pittsburgh Sister Beatrice (not her real name) commented:

We have spiritual and social security all our lives—
who could do better or who would want more?
The confessors are regular, interested in our
spiritual program and willing to help or advise
when requested.

The Rule helps us lead a full, mature spiritual life;
we can't go wrong by observing it. And the
sacrifice of giving up one's own will, as required
by the vow of obedience, takes a greater effort
than exercising one's own will without any
restraint.

To the question asked of sisters in orders in the Cunneen survey: How does your community meet your spiritual
and human needs in its liturgical life? seventy-four percent
answered either "very well" or "adequately." However, all
are not so content. In a response identified as "typical" of another point of view, Sister Monica in Louisville replied:
"The . . . reforms . . . are slow in coming. There is a
conservative element in the community which makes the
going difficult . . . I might add that I'm not the patient
type!"
Sister Dolores, who felt her needs were met poorly
by her religious community, responded:

I'm sorry to be so negative . . . Sisters are told
what to vote when consulted about changes.
Leaving our houses in the evening is *out*. None of
us would dare express an unpopular opinion
publicly on an important issue.

"As it is now," complained Sister Lucy, a postulant
from Rochester,

I can't help but think how much better it *could* be.
We are forbidden to converse with the sisters,
who live and work and eat as separately as
possible. As for confession, I can't turn my
contrition on from 3:45 to 4:15 on Friday
afternoons to a priest who knows me in no other
way.

Sister Consolata expressed the sorrow some of the
older nuns now feel:

The majority of younger sisters are confused and
uncertain about their own vocation, about
fundamental dogma, and about the meaning of the
apostolate. Emphasis on freedom has left many of
them insecure and unhappy.

"The greatest difference," Mrs. Cunneen observes,
"between the sister today and her predecessor is, that whatever position she takes, today's publicity and her sensitivity
to it force her into making it *her* decision."

One of the major decisions facing the frustrated ones
is whether to:

• stay in and *hope* for change
• stay in and *work* for change
• *get out*.

Stay in. Though some, like the impatient Sister Monica, choose to hope, others, like Sister Angela, are determined
to *do* something about it. Eighteen years a teaching nun, she
showed up at a metropolitan "learning to organize" seminar.
"What do you want to organize?" she was asked. Sister

Angela came on strong: "I want to learn to organize *against male domination* in the Church!"

"I have always been excited about being a part of the church," writes a sister-administrator from Milwaukee, "even when I was mad, depressed, disgusted, or disillusioned about what was happening at a given moment, for I am convinced that *even I* can do something about what is happening, and I am determined never to give up trying."

Get out. Ten ex-nuns replied to the Cunneen questionnaire. All, she says, were "non-bitter, objective, and constructive." And all claimed to be following the same purposes they had entered the convent to follow.

How a registered nurse with ten children has any time to give a thought to the Church and the changes she'd like, is uncertain, but here are some of this former sister's hopes and proposals:

- Laity to elect bishops
- Bishops without powers, like the Queen of England
- The Ten Commandments and the precepts of the Church preached as counsels only—for our happiness, not "binding under pain of sin"
- "Roman" and "Catholic" are contradictory—the Holy Spirit breathes on more than Catholics
- Each priest his own rite
- Church property to be taxed
- Laymen to run finances of the Church
- Church to renounce all feudal trappings
- Hierarchy to be called "Alfred"; to become persons instead of officials
- Mass in the homes
- Confession *out*
- No church buildings

- Church not to be worshiped; only God
- Baptism by the parent

And then she concluded, "Well, I can dream!"

In-and-out. One of the surprising twists in the clergy-exit phenomenon is the departure of whole orders which, though now labeled "secular," retain their religious community and turn their disciplined commitment in the direction of social service.

In 1967, forty-four of the Glenmary Sisters of Cincinnati, a small, rural-oriented order, "left" the church to go secular, when they incurred the disapproval of the archbishop who sensed things getting out of control. They now function in Appalachian communities as a service organization, doing social work and teaching.

In Los Angeles, 360 sisters of the Immaculate Heart of Mary set a new numbers-record in Roman Catholic history for defection. When they began to give up their habits and take other jobs, Cardinal McIntyre ordered them back. They appealed to Rome, which insisted they obey him. Their formal statement of withdrawal announced simultaneously the formation of a new secular community, which would be open to married and single persons "who are committed to the service of man in the spirit of the Gospel."

Sister Anita Caspary, president of the order and now the new Immaculate Heart Community president, explained:

> We don't like to sign out, but there is nothing we can do about it. We are not leaving the church. But new forms, new styles, are called for. Under our program, community is approached primarily as a spiritual kinship, rather than as surface uniformity or regimentation.

In the effort to discover "the degree of readiness for change" among sisters in Roman Catholic orders, following Vatican II, a cross-sectional study was commissioned by the Conference of Major Superiors of Women Religious in the United States, in 1965. Sister Marie Augusta Neal, S.N.D., sociologist and director of the survey, reported on the basis of her 139,000 questionnaire replies—an amazing ninety-two percent response—that more than half (sixty-four percent) of the sisters in health, education, and welfare orders were, by then (1970), "change-oriented."

Pandora's Score Card

From the sidelines one may ask: Is the frustrated female making it? In bits and pieces, the answer begins to come. The tip of the iceberg emerges: Mrs. Cynthia Wedel was elected (1969) as the first woman president of the National Council of Churches. Other surfacings, small but significant (significant, also, that these should be thought newsworthy!):

- Women serving as ushers at St. Olaf Catholic Church in downtown Minneapolis. Announced Father Fleming gravely: "The practice of having men only serve as ushers is one of long standing in the Church, but like other customs that have come to impede rather than promote worship, it is time for a change."
- The first "ladies auxiliary" to an order of nuns, a lay group to "live in" a community house with Franciscan Sisters, as a kind of Peace Corps, in Wheaton, Illinois.
- For the first time, women will "count" in making up a *minyan* (the minimum of ten adult Jews that, by ancient custom, constitutes a quorum for Jew-

ish public worship) in Minneapolis (again), in Congregation Adath Jeshurun.

- First woman ever to serve on the faculty at Louisville Presbyterian Theological Seminary: Dr. Catherine Lee Gunsalus.
- First woman diocesan chancellor in the Church of England: Sheila M. Cameron.
- A nun replaces a bishop in the Detroit archdiocese: Sister Mary Corinne Bart, R.S.M. of the Mercy Order. Her assistant will be a priest.

A fresh breeze is blowing. The first authoritative statement of rules governing church life and worship to be published since 1603 in the Church of England (Code of Canons) has issued a new catalog after twenty years of work. Here, it is decreed that the garb of women in the church "shall be suitable to the office and such as to be a sign and mark of holy calling and ministry."

The woman is also "required to swear obedience to the bishop," but she is now granted entry into lay readership, always a carefully guarded male preserve. Women who can pass the test of being able to read and speak "plainly, distinctly, audibly, and reverently" in public may now be licensed to assist the clergy in the Prayer Book services of the Church of England.

Some of her hopes—even preposterous ones—begin to come true. Three years after the former nun dreamed of a church renouncing its feudal trappings, the Vatican announced (April, 1969) by decree of Pope Paul, that "sashes, embroidered in gold, will disappear in ecclesiastical ranks"; that the cardinals' red shoes with silver buckles will be eliminated; and that henceforth the traditional form of address: "I bow to kiss your purple," will be discontinued.

Clergywomen

The theme of this book is clergy. The theme of this chapter is women. We can postpone it no longer: what about clergywomen?

For whatever reasons, women have played a minor role in clerical history. Except for institutions which feature them, such as Christian Science which was founded by a woman, women clergy is a topic that has rather consistently been shoved to the back of the bus.

"Female emancipation" notwithstanding, the religious leader stereotype is traditionally male. Even in the bosom of the church where feminine, maternal traits, such as caring, comforting, and nurturing are called for, the father-image prevails. Moreover, in many traditions, women are *explicitly* prohibited from assuming clergy roles, for example, the Roman Catholic, Greek Orthodox, Anglican, Episcopal, Southern Baptist, and Lutheran religions.

An Anglican church in China once erred in ordaining a woman "by urgent wartime need of her services," but this was later "deplored" by the church authorities and she was asked "not to take advantage of it."

In 1961 the Protestant Episcopal Church in the United States granted permission to woman lay readers to preach, teach, and read parts of the communion service, but *not* to administer the sacraments or receive ordination.

Ordination, in the opinion of one irate woman, a would-be Episcopal priest, is the sticking point. Women can be missionaries and religious teachers—where, she finds, they are usually sidetracked, "but the crunch comes at the altar. The big question is who they're going to let get dressed up and get up there to celebrate the Eucharist."

A Roman Catholic nun in California recently petitioned her bishop for ordination. He said he would be happy to oblige "as soon as Canon Law permits it." Somewhat bitterly she quipped: "In five hundred years, maybe?"

Mrs. Betty Schiess, an active Episcopal church worker in Syracuse, New York, intends to challenge the bishop who declared that "ordaining women would sound the death knell of the church." Now a seminarian in Colgate–Rochester Divinity School, she has ambitions to be the first woman priest of the Episcopal Church. She would also "like to be a bishop." It is her hope that by the time she gets her degree, the church will have mended its ways. Says she:

> The Eucharist is the one act the church performs that it can say no other group performs, and it is the one thing that men have reserved for their very own. Until that is opened up, the rest is just talk.

Some religions do not expressly forbid the ordaining of women, but prevent it by the weight of tradition. Though its theologians have officially found that there is no scriptural reason against it, the Reformed Church in America does not ordain women.

Such also is the case in Judaism. With a centuries-old heritage of a solely male clerical role, bolstered heavily still by contemporary opinion, no woman has ever been called "rabbi." "Technically," says Conservative Professor Seymour Siegel of Jewish Theological Seminary, "there is no reason why a woman can't be a rabbi, except for the mores of ancient times." However, were she ordained, declares an Orthodox rabbi, she probably would not be recognized as such by Jews. "It doesn't matter what they call her. And it would never be repeated."

In this tradition, also, a woman is determined to crack the barrier. Sally Priesand, who has "wanted to be a rabbi since the tenth grade," is enrolled at Hebrew Union College in Cincinnati. In the ninety-five–year history of the college, seven women have entered the study program, but so far, Miss Priesand has held on the longest. The reason for most of the others dropping out was that they became convinced that Jews, even Reform Jews of the liberal wing, were not yet ready for women rabbis.

Churches are gradually loosening prohibitions against ordaining women. In 1956, the Methodist Church in the United States granted women full clergy rights, and the United Presbyterians began ordaining women. The Brethren have ordained women since 1960. In 1966, the Episcopal Church appointed a national committee to "study the proper place of women in the Church's ministry." In 1970, the national convention of the Lutheran Church of America authorized its synods to ordain women.

However, others like Mrs. Schiess have discovered to their sorrow that repealing laws against female ordination does not necessarily turn the trick. Churches may permit it in principle but avoid it in practice. Again, a woman who is ordained may find there are "no available openings."

Elsie Thomas Culver, a Congregationalist and one of the few ordained women ministers in America, is Director of Public Relations for the World Council of Churches. In that capacity, she took a poll of tradition and practices. She notes, for example, that the Methodist Church has for some time now ordained women "but without any assurance of appointment." As of 1963, she reports, there were 380 ordained Methodist women, but "only a few" were ministers in churches. Much the same can be said of other churches which ordain women in this country.

Even in denominations where clergywomen are permitted, the possibility is rarely envisioned by their laymen. Should the question arise, it is seen as a preposterous, even revolting, state of affairs.

Here the parallel between women and blacks is quite striking. In 1967, a continental poll of Unitarian Universalists found that 47.2% of them felt a woman minister's sex "might hamper her effectiveness." Only 26.6% said this might be true of a Negro minister; indeed, 10.9% said "his race might improve his effectiveness." Black senior ministers serving white congregations are still so rare as simply to prove the rule.

Black ministers as one of a team in white or predominantly white churches are becoming fashionable, though blacks are understandably skeptical whether both team members are thought of as equals. But women have even farther to go: one hears almost nothing of male/female teams except from patronizing parsons who are blind to the issue and speak of "my team." The reason is that such a "team" is uniformly a male superiority stereotype: in churches, women are firmly boxed into the role of secretary, or education director (at a third the salary and less than half the status of the pastor).

White racism and male domination deny full personhood to non-whites and non-males. They have been accepted as "natural" by the dominant strain of our culture. This is why, for those who do the dominating, they are so hard to perceive, let alone change. But because it rests on denial and repression, the status of blacks and women in the church has never been secure. A look at history shows that their gains are rather recent, and costly.

To this day, bubbling up through and around established churches, there are mystical, spiritual cults, not infrequently led by women. These are in the tradition of the earth-religions, dominant in the ancient world, which celebrated the feminine rather than the masculine side of humanness.

The Bible records that in emerging Judaism, oracle and seer and priestess, along with fertility-cults, were suppressed and scattered by the inconceivably great (but definitely male) Jehovah–God. The Jews, however, were a tiny minority.

Early Christianity, springing from Judaism, found itself surrounded by a sea of mother-goddess religions. It fought a long, touch-and-go battle with them. Maleness and rationality won. This victory expressed itself in the Trinity concept, which in its exclusiveness is the quintessence of male theologizing. There is no place for the feminine in Father, Son, and Holy Ghost.

Woman however, like water her symbol, is as persistent as she is fluid. The Church found it could not deny, or do without, a Mother Mary. The earth-mother religions threatened to flow into official Christianity in her wake. Filtered through the male intellect, Mary became the Queen of Heaven, the Virgin, the pure.

While Mary saved the day by preserving the feminine qualities, under a male-dominated theology those qualities were outside as competitors, rather than being integrated with the masculine. Thus, the male libido, unchecked, burst forth in centuries of aggression (the fruits of conquest were, of course, offered to Mother Church). Again, in this polarization are discernible the beginnings of our double standard. The dominant western religion has never known how to manage sex or aggression.

Through these ages, Mary was understood by the common folk as merciful to fallen women, and to other transgressors against the male-constructed machinery of sinfulness and penitence. Some psychologists contend that her cult, which today has elevated her almost (but not quite) to equality with the Persons of the Trinity, manifests a "racial unconscious" in which femaleness asserts itself. At any rate, the feminine element cannot be denied or downgraded except at the price of cultural sickness.

The scriptural justification for male supremacy, usually cited by both Protestants and Catholics, is Timothy I, ii, 11–13:

> Women are to keep silence, and take their place
> with all submissiveness as learners. A woman shall
> have no leave from me to teach, and to issue
> commands to her husband. Her part is to be silent.

In the words of a Catholic woman teaching in a mid-west university:

> No amount of rhapsodizing about women's nature
> as a "complement to man" can get us away from
> these two basic limitations: the social conditions of
> the Jewish world at the time of Christ and St.
> Paul; and the scholastic philosophy of the
> thirteenth century, both of which circumscribed
> them. Only changes in canon law can do that.

Moreover, she adds that she is a part of the church

> only to the extent that I can receive the
> sacraments. I feel that the church's restriction
> against the participation of women keeps me from
> being a *full* member.

An interdenominational American Association of Women Ministers has been formed to give encouragement to present and prospective female clergy. They number at present about three hundred members. One item of cheer supplied by their director of research, Dr. Hazel E. Foster, a United Church of Christ minister, is that Paul was not the author of the Biblical directive for women "to keep silence" in the churches.

The executive board of the Association urged the

Consultation on Church Union (COCU) to include ordination of women in all deliberations on church union.

There is, then, a sprinkling of women ministers, or "women who are ministers" as some of them prefer to be known, dispersed through the clerical echelons of a few denominations.

The Universalist Church of America was a notable exception to the usual pattern, even among the more liberal religions. From a very early period it had women ministers and admitted women to its theological schools. Maria Cook was the first to hold a Universalist preaching license, in 1811, in the state of New York. Even so, it is recorded that she felt she was not cordially received by her brother ministers, and after a few months tore up her license.

The Universalist Church, says its historian Clinton Lee Scott, probably had a larger proportion of women ministers than any in America. There have been at one time as many as seventy in good standing, most of whom were in settled pastorates, i.e. about twenty percent of the ministers on their list.

In her history of Universalism in Iowa, Dorothy Grant reports that women as well as men, and quite on a par with men, rode the circuits, founded churches, filled the pulpits, and "manned" the preaching stations. "Even before Iowa had become a territory in the late 1830's, more than thirty Universalist men and women were traveling through fifty communities to establish preaching sites. . . ." The Universalists' attitude toward women was expressed by a Rev. Mr. E. Manford thus:

> Let woman speak as well as man in the lecture
> room and even in the pulpit. Let her speak on all
> subjects of human interest. As she belongs to the
> human family, she is as much interested as man
> in all intellectual and moral subjects.

Precarious Perch

Standard ministers in standard churches have great areas of uncertainty and ambivalent zones of role conflict. The female minister lives in a sort of double limbo: the uncertain and undefined parameters of femaleness and female occupation, within the ill-defined context of ministerial profession. How does one talk to a minister? How does one talk to him if he's a girl?

The rarity of her breed, the novelty of her situation, stand in the way of optimal effectiveness. As things are, she spends an inordinate amount of time and energy just rehearsing "what it's like to be a lady minister."

When she comes as a candidate before a ministerial selection committee, the question "Why do *you* want to be a minister?" takes precedence over "What kind of minister are you?" On her candidating statement to a selection committee in 1962, the Rev. Violet Kochendoerfer declared:

> *I enter the ministry as a woman, but hope to be accepted as a person.*
>
> I do not feel I must prove anything. I am not a feminist. I look to the ministry as a mutual endeavor. . . . The real question is not, *Do you want a woman minister*, but Do you want *me* as a minister.

The frustration is comparable to that experienced in an interracial marriage, that is, the couple is so busy answering questions about "what it's like" to be married to one of a different race, that there is little time left for experiencing it.

To have survived abrasive internships and bull sessions in the masculine halls of seminaries, and cut a track

through the competition for a pulpit, takes a strong and determined person, annealed to an inner toughness.

The selection process screens for aggressive and as-
sertive "male-type" characteristics in ministerial students who
are women. These tough-minded colleagues are a bit jolting
to male divinity students, whose own profile tends, as we
shall see, to emphasize "female," even passive-dependent
characteristics. In the words of a seminarian who seriously
opposes Miss Priesand's plans to become a rabbi: "I like
Sally, *but*. . . . Intellectually, I can say 'Go ahead—we're
liberal.' Emotionally, though, I don't like it."

Though she spins in an endless whirl of people—
meetings, committees, socials—her greatest problem may be
loneliness. If, like pert Rev. Emma Lou, she's unmarried, she
may feel:

> There's just no way out. I can't date single men
> in the congregation—that would upset the parish
> and wreck my clergy relations. I can't go with
> men outside: being a 'reverend' doesn't help. I'm
> always set apart.

Going and coming, the stereotypes get her. The
"woman in religion" is supposed to be an education director
or Sunday School teacher and finds herself almost inevitably
identified as such, directed and steered by officialdom to this
predetermined end. If she does convince people this is not
her dish, and makes it to the pulpit, she's framed in square expectations of goodyness, separateness, nonhumanness.

Her dilemma: to admit and discuss the problem in
her parish, brings attention to what is already uncomfortable,
and feeds her growing appearance and/or sense of paranoia.
To try to avoid the subject only builds the tension.

Whatever the principles involved, women are sometimes better qualified and often temperamentally better

suited for ministering than men. Even for *ad*-ministering! "I can say things men can't say" says rabbi-candidate Sally. "I'm able to work on people to make them change their minds. People tell me that I remember to do things, like details, that men don't think about."

They may have been shortchanged, in salary and in title and status, but behind thousands of churches and temples have stood just such back-of-the-scene executives and administrators, church secretaries and wives.

Lady Dropouts

The total number of female clergy, in denominations which permit them, is so small that study samples drawn from these are scarcely definitive. What data we have, however, are highly suggestive.

There were four dropout clergywomen in the United Church of Christ *Ex-Pastors* research. Three of these regard the problems of being a woman professional as *central* to their reasons for leaving the church. Some verbatim comments:

- I'm not welcome at ministers' meetings.
- No one wants me on a team.
- What do we do with a woman minister or any member of a minority group? I haven't advanced to the degree I should. I'll be on this level forever.
- I do all the dirty work.
- I can't be a professional woman in the church. I want to be a professional woman.
- . . . people are politer—but . . . a single woman needs a full-time salary.
- I never learned to knuckle under to the male ego.

Three of the four in this sample are seminary graduates. All four are unmarried. One added sympathetically: "Single men also have a hard time."

In its "control" sample of female clergy still in the parish, the same study discovered one lady minister who was "satisfied and adjusted." She was eighty years old.

Another, with a thirty-five-year history of small-town pastorates, gives *extremely* low rating (her italics) "to clergy, peers, and denominational executives as part of the support system."

A third, a young seminary graduate who is married to a minister, now plans to enter a secular field. She, also, regards fellow-clergy and denominational executives as "unsupportive and highly isolating." Serious problems also are interprofessional communication and salary.

In passing, one must note: if ambiguity clouds the role of female clergy, it is *nothing* to the no man's land of the clergywoman's spouse! Perhaps he may have it all worked out, like Nancy Stratton's husband (not her real name): well established in his profession, he is able, and willing, to make and break work ties according to the pattern of *her* successive moves from congregation to congregation and city to city. In all likelihood, he's the only one so adjustable.

However, in a reverse switch on women's liberation, one ministers' wives' association, in 1970, voted to explore the possibility of expanding its membership to include *men* who are "the spouses of women clergy."

For the future, it seems safe to assume that we haven't heard the last from the girls. Presumably, by the time Bishop Betty and Rabbi Sally and some of their friends have been ordained and installed, the novelty and self-consciousness will have faded. Then, perhaps, the possibility of and possibilities for women clergy will begin to open up in non-packaged, creative ways.

CHAPTER SIX

Holy Matrimony

It was bound to happen sooner or later. Sex has hit the church. Magazines and TV, movies and the stage—that's one thing. But the citadel of purity, the church—that's something else!

It's obviously a problem for Catholics: almost every day there is an item about a priest who marries or a squabble over birth control. But it isn't just a Catholic problem. Only the versions are different.

"Our most serious problem, and the toughest to deal with," said a thoughtful rabbi, "is intermarriage. How should we handle it? What should we do?"

Earnest Protestants, with their Puritan hangups, worry as much these days about the state of marriage as they do about the state of the church.

Pushed by technology on the one hand, with its pills and ads and media; by the human revolution on the other, with its new frontiers of freedom, equality, sexuality, and self-realization—from both sides it comes. The church is caught squarely between them. The issue is embarrassing and ubiquitous; too hot to handle but insistent.

To Marry or to Burn

If there were nothing else in the works but the celibacy issue, there would be fuel enough to keep Rome heated for many a day. The "issue" refers not to priests alone, but to nuns, brothers, bishops—any and all in the orders, parishes, and institutions of the church who have taken the vow of chastity. It boils down essentially to the question whether individuals on their own may depart from the celibate state which the church in its wisdom has established, and to which they have solemnly agreed. The Vatican states: "The Latin rite Church has given the rule . . . of choosing for the priesthood only those who are willing freely to embrace celibacy for the sake of the Kingdom of Heaven."

Celibacy has always been a problem; there have always been transgressions: "The public does not know that they happen, but the priests do," comments Pierre Hermand, in *The Priest: Celibate or Married?* Church spokesmen are wont to embroider celibacy with flourishes of rhetoric, as "a surpassing gift of grace," or "a gift from Christ," or "this great jewel in the crown of the Church." But, Hermand says, "The Latin priesthood lives by a tradition which has never been made the object of a profound and critical examination." Instead, it is simply proclaimed by *fiat:* "Celibacy," said Pope Paul, "is a capital law of our Latin Church. It cannot be abandoned or put into discussion."

Three Sides of the Issue. To get hold of the subject, one must turn it around in several ways.

Side One is that of the church, the traditional loyal view. In Hermand's words, ". . . celibacy liberates the priest who, if he were married, could not dedicate himself so fully to his mission."

A Jesuit sociologist, Joseph Sanders, reviews the traditional argument as follows:

One, it is an imitation of Christ and a following of His counsel in the Gospel to 'renounce the companionship of marriage for the sake of the Kingdom.'

Two, it is a devoting of oneself to the Lord with an undivided love, since one is not simultaneously solicitous for a wife and children.

Three, it is a style of life by which the priest bears witness to the state which the resurrection of the body will bring about in the world to come, that is, where there will be no marriage.

Four, it is a way by which the priest gains extremely appropriate help for exercising that perfect and unremitting love by which he can become all things to all men through his priestly ministration. That is, he is totally available and mobile for his apostolate.

The second "side" is the rebuttal to the traditional position, that is, the disloyal view, which asks: "What kind of man does it produce?" Hermand answers: "Men with psychological problems of all types." He says, "The celibate priest can't be taken as a full person; only a marginal one. He has difficulty relating humanly and giving human advice."

Says Arthur LeBlanc, former Paulist priest, "I have no doubt that many men find in an open, mature, and loving religious community, all the support that they need to lead useful and rewarding lives. Some, however, will find that they require the attention and devotion found only in the marital state."

These words, and the testaments of the other eleven

men in *Why Priests Leave*, are an eloquent refutation of the church's position.

But there is a third side, too. Whatever the theological rationale for it may be, celibacy is a key ingredient of the glue which has held the Church of Rome together.

Celibacy promotes the important function of "institutional severance" which separates church personnel from the outside world physically, psychologically, and symbolically. Its closest parallel is an army, which must be set apart from the rest of society. On this pattern the Jesuits were modeled. The celibate priest is indoctrinated, uniformed, under orders. His "home leaves" are severely restricted. In addition, whereas the soldier, though separated from civilians, is not regarded as superior to them, the celibate priest is looked to as a higher order of person.

Celibacy reduces, almost eliminates, competition with other institutions. With no ties, no relationships, responsibilities or commitments, it obviates rival demands. With no spouse, no children, there is no one to inherit anything a priest acquires for, or is given for, the church. The celibate state promotes singleness and intensity of purpose.

It is a powerful mechanism of control. Removal of outside persons and loyalties, affections and sex, along with marriage to the church, reduces the excuse for, and the opportunity for, privacy. It is a simple, straight line: all loyalty and obedience to the church, all discipline in a clear line from it.

Henry Charles Lea sums it up, in his study of sacerdotal celibacy. The canon which bound all the active pastors of the church to perpetual celibacy "created an impassable barrier between them and the outer world," which was in turn "one of the efficient instruments in erecting and consolidating both the spiritual and temporal power of the Roman hierarchy."

The First 1900 Years. The Catholic clergy did not start as celibate. This feature, like so many under fire today (papal infallibility, or the very recent anti-birth control position) came from the evolving culture rather than from original Christianity.

In the first four centuries of the church, Father Sanders notes, there were always some few people—it is hard to determine how many—who practiced celibacy and were highly thought of in the community. In the early centuries, however, almost nothing was written about it. The Council of Elvira (305 A.D.) and the Council of Arles (314 A.D.) both legislated to the effect that men in holy orders in the Western Church should not have intercourse with their wives. By the time of St. Leo the Great (440–461) clerical celibacy had become obligatory throughout the West.

After the fifth century, the concept of being celibately "married to the church" was reiterated and reinforced by pope after pope until our own times. In 1918 the Code of Canon Law, Section I, declared that "Clerics in major orders cannot contract matrimony. They are bound to observe chastity in such a manner that to sin against chastity constitutes a sacrilege." In 1935, Pope Pius XI published his encyclical *Ad Catholicii Sacerdotii*, which reaffirmed celibacy for the priesthood. In 1954, Pope Pius XII issued an encyclical entitled *Sacra Virginitas* which praised virginity as being superior to married life.

However, there were rumblings from below. In 1959, it was openly suggested that persons might be admitted to minor orders and even to the subdiaconate, without the full obligations of the priesthood: perhaps, without the requirement of celibacy. An Italian theologian, Fr. Spiazzi, went so far as to open the possibility of married priests—a suggestion which met with no warm reception.

Galled by "the hypocrisy and scandal in the Church" Father Hermand wrote his book. In 1965, he relates,

> I showed the pages to some priests. All of them recognized that the problems raised were real ones and painful ones. One of them, an eminent theologian, said to me, 'The problem is real, very real. No one wants to study it, however.' Nearly all advised against publishing this work.
>
> The ordinary faithful are not ready for this upheaval, for calling celibacy into question. Nor is the hierarchy ready to accept the fact that the initiation, in the debate, is taken at a lower level. The weight of tradition is too heavy; the problems of love and sexuality which are inevitably raised all along the way, are much too *tabu*. 'You will only cause confusion,' I was told, 'and destroy any remaining confidence the people have in their priests. Some priests will take advantage of your book to give up their celibacy. You will hinder those who are preparing the ground for a better and more mature statement of the question.'

Hermand could not get permission for the book, and left the priesthood to publish it.

At almost the same time, *The National Catholic Reporter*, one of the more daring Catholic publications, released an article entitled "Should the Council Look at Celibacy?" (Vatican II was then in session.) This marked the real beginning of public debate on the issue in the United States and of a growing literature on the subject.

However, Pope Paul would not open debate on the topic at the Council. He reserved the question of celibacy to himself. On June 24, 1967, he issued the encyclical *Priestly*

Celibacy. Many were surprised that the encyclical was issued prior to the convening of the synod of bishops in Rome. The Pope himself had earlier appointed a commission of almost ninety members from around the world: experts in theology, sociology, biology, and so on, to consider the problem and to advise all concerned on the knotty dilemma. The encyclical paid tribute to the "sweet burden of sacerdotal chastity" but did nothing to relieve that burden. Since then, debate has waxed loud and hot.

The Vatican issued another statement (August, 1969) through John Cardinal Wright, prefect of the Sacred Conference of the Clergy: "There will be no change in the Roman Catholic requirement of clerical celibacy in the immediate future." The U.S. bishops fell into line a few months later, saying that compulsory celibacy is "profoundly appropriate" for priests.

Ever more vocal counter-movements are springing up. Notable among these is the National Association for Pastoral Renewal (NAPR), an organization of priests (both in and outside the church), and a few laypersons, formed with the objective of reforming the celibacy rule.

In the opinion of its first national coordinator, Robert Duggan, celibacy is "*the* issue today for the Roman Church." The Church, he says, "can't even begin to deal with other issues until it solves this one."

The position of the bishops, Duggan explains, is that celibacy is not discussable. Actually, he points out, the problem is not so much to get the bishops to change. Nor even the local priests: every survey in the United States taken among diocesan priests in the last several years has shown at least forty percent of them coming out for optional celibacy, especially the younger ones.

The solid wall behind the bishops' stand is the laity. Many lay Catholics are astonished to discover that celibacy is being questioned. "Priests just don't marry." Said a store clerk: "I wouldn't go to a priest if he didn't keep his vows. If he doesn't keep his vows, what would mine be worth?"

A Catholic news reporter asks: "What's his beef? He knew what he was getting into when he signed up."

The National Association for Pastoral Renewal is not out to repeal celibacy, but to make it optional. And optional celibacy is not a mere matter of changing the rules, Duggan, a former priest, now married, points out.

> It has far broader and deeper implications: it has to do with one's facing and understanding his own sexuality, i.e. his identity, his self-image, his personhood. Facing up to the whole person, and his freedom as a person—really, it calls for re-making the self. . . . Only through the celibacy issue can you get at all the other issues in the Church. . . . The key to it is putting personal values above those of the institution. . . . Isn't it ironical that these priests are just discovering marriage as Margaret Mead announces that the institution of marriage is dying!

Second Verse, Same as the First

The flap over birth control is virtually a facsimile of the celibacy ruckus. First comes the traditional "no-no" stand of the church. Then the grumbles. Then an encyclical laying down the law. Then hell to pay.

The most publicized blowup in the United States came when forty priests in Washington, D.C., refused to accept Pope Paul's encyclical on birth control. Penalties or no penalties, said they, it was a matter of conscience. There were penalties: Cardinal O'Boyle suspended them, in September, 1968. Declared O'Boyle: "A Catholic forms his conscience in the light of what the Church teaches, in the sense that he forms it in accordance with what the Church teaches. . . . We can be sure that the Church will not contradict herself on contraception." The Pope backed him up: as the international press reported, "Only rarely does the Vatican Radio carry so many excerpts from a prelate's talk." Pope Paul publicly commended O'Boyle and urged the forty priests to knuckle under.

But in Washington it became a *cause célèbre*. At the semiannual meeting of the National Conference of Catholic Bishops, there were petitions presented from more than 10,000 Catholics of the area protesting the suspension. An association of Detroit priests sent their support. Five nuns met with the Cardinal on behalf of the area superintendent of schools, who was one of the forty.

The wife of Senator Philip Hart, of Michigan, said she was "appalled" at the suspension, and offered her home as a temporary sanctuary for the priests. Mrs. Hart was "dismayed by the Pope's encyclical." Parents, she went on, "must have the freedom of conscience to determine when and how many children they will have."

Here again, an organization resulted: the Center for Christian Renewal. Mrs. Hart was chairman. Concerned laymen purchased a building as headquarters, and as a temporary residence for priests turned out of their rectories. It was also announced, that if there were no success in getting the bishops to intercede on behalf of the forty, the Center would become a clearing-house for getting them jobs.

The identical pattern of back-and-forth declaration and petition was reenacted among the Dutch Catholics, where theologians, priests, bishops, and finally, laity joined in the fight. The Dutch petitioned against both birth control and celibacy. They too were doubly refused. In February, 1970, the Pope replied that henceforth, Roman Catholic priests would be asked to reaffirm their vows of celibacy and obedience, not once, for life, but *once a year*.

Fighting the Wrong War

The last word has not been spoken on birth control or on celibacy. In both cases, furthermore, a crucial and significant fact is now coming to light: though both *seem* to be centered in sex, underlying them both are quite different issues.

In a number of "defections for reasons of celibacy," it turns out that this is not actually and honestly the issue. James J. Gill, a Jesuit priest and doctor on the staff of the Harvard University health services, says on the basis of about a hundred interviews of priests who have left: "It is incorrect to assume that celibacy is in and of itself a major causal factor in the decision." It is Dr. Gill's opinion, backed up by others, that marriage is, for the unhappy, confused, and questing priest, a *result* and symptom of his unhappiness and frustration. Often, he explains,

> some sensitive woman perceives his deep need for someone to love him, not for his performance or accomplishments, but for his own sake. He responds with gratitude and love. She has brought a kind of joy he never knew until now. She has lifted him at least part way out of his state of depression and he feels he can't afford to lose her.

Father Gill emphasizes that, paradoxical as it seems, the basic problem of the priest who leaves the ministry has nothing at all to do with sex. The woman is, in effect, a therapist. "When he finds a woman who will give him love," he explains, "not for what he accomplishes, but for what he is, he becomes capable of respecting himself again."

Sociologist Fr. Eugene Schallert's inquiry supports these conclusions. Many priests think they leave to marry, he reports, but actually leave for other reasons. His survey suggests that the restless priest moves through a certain sequence. First he begins to ask, Who am I? He seeks help from someone whom Fr. Schallert calls "the crucial other" —a close friend, superior, or confessor. When he does not get the help he seeks, he decides to leave. *Once that decision is made*, he may develop a close relationship with a woman. "When we get around to talking with him about it, the thing on his mind is the woman. Then, we start probing to find when this all started, and discover that it wasn't a woman at all."

So, what many are opposing, even through the celibacy reform organizations, is not celibacy as such, but *compulsory* celibacy. Nor are they insisting on marriage, but on the freedom to choose marriage. The issue is one of *options*. In the same way, those attempting to change the official stand on birth control are insisting on the right of parents to *choose* how many children they will have.

If all this is correct, then this is the wrong war: the villain of the piece is not the vow of chastity, but the vow of obedience.

The difference is crucial, and provides clues to other puzzling developments. Why, for example, Protestant clergy would take on the vow of celibacy, just as Catholics are so vigorously throwing it over. The answer, of course: the Protestant who makes that decision—a small number, it is true—does so voluntarily. It also explains why the leaders of "celibacy reform" are not pushing for its repeal. Their target is not celibacy, but the freedom to decide.

And why are the motives being given by so many defectors held in question? Consciously or unconsciously, they are not coming clean. The real reason is not celibacy at all, but something else. They are using this current and easily grasped issue as an excuse and ready "out." Their desires for more freedom and choice in an authoritarian church are less easy to explain and in the light of long tradition, to justify.

Perhaps even too overwhelming for them to talk about.

Obviously the authorities can no longer stem the tide. Even "good" Catholics no longer pay much attention to what their church says on such matters. More and more, laity are doing what individually they feel is right.

The question is, when will the crumbling wall of church authority (on the issues of chastity and obedience) topple over completely?

The Pair in the Parsonage

Turning now to that placid oasis, the parsonage, where the Pope does not enter, celibacy is no problem, and there are no vows of chastity, what do we find? Nothing less than that marriage is a problem if you have it and a problem if you don't.

Catholic priests fight to marry. Protestant clergy *have* to. Both are stuck with a phony image and a counsel of perfection: one of celibacy, the other of marriage. To pretend that either works according to the rhetoric or rules is hypocrisy.

The Catholic Church imposes celibacy. What happens? A vast pretense. Covering up for the myriads of transgressions are double lives, cheating, concealing, and fear. As for the Protestants' holy state of matrimony, says Charles M. Smith, the Methodist satirist:

> You will find it expedient to pretend that you
> dwell in a state of marital bliss . . . (although)
> the nervous strain involved in such pretensions is of
> awesome proportions, and is known to have
> pushed parsonage wives into emotional breakdowns
> and turned parsonage children into church-hating
> delinquents.

One of that rare breed, a lady "clergyman" tells of leaving her pastorate and ending her marriage at the same time. When she sought a new pulpit, the executive of her "liberal" denomination said, "The divorce is no problem. Your being single is. When you get married again, we'll talk about finding a new job." If the parson has not married her earlier to type his thesis, or to put him through seminary, he *must* find someone when he takes a church. The reason, once more from that tongue-in-cheek observer, Smith: "The folklore of the trade holds that it is necessary for a minister to marry in order to set an example of Christian family life. The real reasons why you should marry are, of course, not at all related to the folklore." He goes on:

First, a clergyman who remains unmarried for more than a year after graduation from seminary is suspected of being abnormal, immoral, or chicken.

Second, there will be those who will speculate that he has taken St. Paul on marriage too seriously, and has made a secret vow of celibacy. As far as your parishioners are concerned, you may be as celibate as a Cistercian monk, but they will insist that you practice it within the married state.

Third, somewhat more than half of your congregation will be women, and all women: single, married, widowed (including grass widows), resent a male eligible for marriage who chooses to remain unwed.

Fourth, and here is the over-riding argument in the mind of the congregation, since the church owns a parsonage, and already has arrived at a salary figure below which it cannot go and maintain its conviction, however illusory, that it is a humane institution, it is only sensible to get two employees for the price of one. Therefore it boils down to a business proposition. It would be damaging and vulgar to admit to this, however, so the tradition and the folklore was manufactured to mask it.

. . . . .

Actually, it is very good business from the church's point of view. Most girls are piano players of sorts, and anyone can learn to operate a typewriter or mimeograph. Add to these . . . a miscellany of other small parish chores, all of which your wife will be expected in your first small parishes to perform . . . and you have a job analysis which, were it filled by a salaried employee, would require no small addition to the annual budget. Hence the tradition of a parish clergy.

With all these external institutional pressures to marry, many parsons marry, or stay married, for the wrong reasons. When the strain grows to be just too much, they leave the pulpit to divorce.

At this point we hit the double standard. In Protestantism, laity are permitted to divorce, but not the clergy. As a consultant said to a group of ministers at a conference: "Professionally, divorce is disastrous. Divorce is not open to *you*, and you'd better know it." Says an officer of a clergy association:

For our clergy, divorce is a built-in prohibition. It is a matter of unwritten professional ethics, to lay one's resignation before his board, if he wants to obtain a divorce. There are other escape hatches, though. The divorcing minister doesn't have to leave the church. He can go elsewhere in the denomination, just so he's 'out of sight' of the parish. Many of those ending up in national posts are divorced.

Placement officers of the very liberal Unitarian Universalists note that, though some now "get away with it," most divorcing ministers find they must move within a year, because of local pressures and criticism. Furthermore, such moves can usually be only "lateral"—that is, toward a congregation of equal or lesser prominence.

There is undoubtedly a marked increase of divorce among clergy. In 1964 Scherer's study of United Church pastors found only 2.2% divorced or separated. By 1969 the figure had risen to 11.8%. At least one straw in the wind signals a change: that divorce is coming to be accepted as normal, and in many cases, as more good than bad. Rev. Rudolph Nemser of Fairfax, Virginia, is preparing a handbook on divorce for use with children. His reason: because we regard divorce as shameful, we say as little as we can about it. Yet for today's children, broken families are almost the rule. Nemser found, when he started to ask young people about their attitudes, he was the first adult who had given them an opportunity to talk. He is one of a number of ministers working on a "divorce service," a religious ceremony for that serious moment in people's lives, the *un*tying of the marital knot. "To be sure, people aren't ready for this as yet," he says, "but I think we'll come to it."

Why the upswing in clergy divorce? There are several reasons: among them, of course, a general loosening up of attitudes in society at large. But there are more specific reasons among clergy. The perfection image of ministerial marriage is simply unsupportable. Also, both from within himself and from his people, too, there is pressure to accept the parson as a person, with human, even marital, problems. Equally important are factors having to do with his wife.

Shadow of a Shadow

Look at the minister's wife! Few people do. His role is uncertain? That's *nothing* to hers! She is tied to his kite, and his kite is wavering. Her role is to abet someone whose role is in doubt. She has no place to stand. She is always "the parson's wife," not Madge or Mary or Mabel. Not the artist or the teacher, the person, but the one who occupies the role that shores up the parson, whose role is uncertain. She's a "person" twice or thrice removed, the shadow of a shadow. When she rises up, as she is bound to some day, we will have the next in the series: the "parson's wife revolution."

One of the few who have looked into her situation is William Douglas, a clergyman who "dropped out" to make this study and who has now returned to the church. Of his return, he says, "I guess I am a deviant." What is striking about Douglas' *Ministers' Wives*, published in 1965, is his finding that the basic image of them has changed so little from what it used to be. He found a book called *Hints for a Clergyman's Wife, or Female Parochial Duties*, published in 1832, which, he says, sets forth pretty much what the expectation not only has been, but, alas, still is. The goal of a parson's spouse should be:

> The advancement of her husband's ministry, the salvation of the souls committed to her pastoral charge, and the alleviation of their temporal wants. Let her feel that, on becoming a clergyman's wife, she has, as it were, wedded herself to her husband's parish, and to the best interest of his flock.

As one present-day inheritor of this formidable stereotype puts it:

> A real dilemma faces the wife of the parson. How

can she raise well-balanced children, how can she
keep abreast of her husband's interests, share his
intellectual search, charm his friends, ward off
predatory females, challenge him, intrigue him,
nurture him, captivate him, and still be her
all-too-human self?

Though Douglas notes "an increasing realization that
ministers' wives have rights as well as duties," nevertheless he
observes that "the cultural image . . . tends to remain that
of a 'poor thing' with little zip, sparkle, or attractiveness,
condemned to a hard life with few elements of fun or comfort."

If the public image of the preacher's wife has changed
surprisingly little over the years, her self-image is changing
rapidly. As Douglas concludes, she is an individual. It is impossible to classify her, as he tried several times to do while
preparing his study. This is something even her well-inten-
tioned friends find difficult to grasp. One sympathetic
churchman wrote an article in which he declared: "Don't
always think of her as 'the *minister's* wife.' Think of her,
rather, as a mother and a wife." But that's off, too! She
doesn't want to be just "Jim's wife" or "Sally's mom" either.
First and foremost, she wants to be herself.

The Vanishing Violet

Reports of two interviewers who have talked with
clergy wives all over the country came up with these conclusions: "She's suffering from 'appendage syndrome,'" and
"She's had it with the once-removed bit." So part of the
word from the parsonage is, the violet is vanishing. She has
had enough of the back seat, and is going to be herself. And
this can mean "or else." No doubt, the minister has more

opportunity to roll a roving eye, as his wife is well aware. One supposes that it is always he who leaves her. But one new study, though it did not seek statistics in the matter, uncovered the fact that in several cases at least, it was the wives, not the ministers, who initiated the divorce action.

"Meekness and humility, quiet endurance and prayer" may have been prime duties and virtues a century ago. But today's wife is important to herself. Furthermore, she is of crucial importance to her minister husband: not just in personal relationship, but in his career. In trying to measure the support system of ministers—a system everyone needs—researchers have found that wives are by far their most supportive associates (75.8% of the ex-pastors in the United Church of Christ study, and 85.2% of the active pastors, rated their wives as "very supportive"). Much to the surprise of these and other researchers in other denominations, his wife's opinion of the minister's professional performance meant more to him than the opinion of anyone else—including that of his peers and superiors!

No wonder, then, that when any reasonably happily married minister—and most are so—finds that the ministry jeopardizes his marriage, he wants out. "*I* found it hard enough to take the guff," said one who left for teaching. "For *her*, it was impossible." The United Church study found that 54.9% of the wives of ex-pastors preferred, or were even eager, to leave the church; only 12.2% wished to stay. In the Unitarian Universalist survey, not one was found who wanted to go back.

The United Church researchers conclude their lengthy discussion of marriage and family factors by saying: "It may seem we have labored the point of showing the influence of family problems, but it appears that ex-pastors scarcely recognize the significance of their family systems in making career decisions." Their last word: "The ministry is a strain even on a strong marriage."

The Double Knot

Somebody always asks: "What's all the fuss? It's the same with the doctor's wife—he's always 'on call.' The lawyer's wife—'I never see him.' The executive's wife—'He's getting ulcers.'" Emphatically and categorically: *This marriage is different.*

In the parish, marriage is a double knot: one is tied to a helpmeet *and* to a church. This imposes pressures and problems far more encompassing than those about which other wives complain.

One special problem is the burden of perfection. Dr. Thomas Osborne, a psychologist in Wheaton, Massachusetts, says that unlike all other professionals, the clergyman and his family are supposed to reflect the "should do's," while the rest of the world goes about with the "do do's." As a layman explained it to a pastor's wife: "We pay you *not* to have problems." Other typical burdens, as seen through the eyes of clergy wives (present and ex), are these:

"The Goldfish Bowl"

I resented having the way I raised my children and conducted myself as a wife, mother, person, and church member, stared at and evaluated by everyone.

"The 24-Hour Day"

It's just that *sharing* goes on twenty-four hours a day, seven days a week. You'd like to get away and can't. Churches eat ministers up!

"No Damned Let-Up"

We never had a vacation . . . much less a day set

aside for ourselves! That 'week-end away' was
always a church conference!

"Always on the Move"

The fact that he is a minister has necessitated our
leaving two homes I would have preferred staying
in . . .

[Adds a minister's son]:

Being a preacher's kid is hard on a guy and his
friendships. Every move, he has to give up his
friends. I haven't any more close friends. You
don't make close friends if you know you'll be
yanked.

"He's Really Theirs"

We are expected to share in candidating (in one
church, I even pre-candidated). We help in the
church school (or direct it—I did). We pour
gallons of coffee, cook mountains of food, are on
call day and night (if the minister is out, they
think I'm hiding him!)—but *our husbands belong
to Them!*

"I Get the Crumbs"

You have to get used to the fact that a minister
can't be expected to give his family a conventional
share of fatherly attention. In actuality married to
the church, he usually gives his flock priority . . .
and his wife has to fend for herself as best she can.

"Too Bad for the Kids"

Our road was paved with unkept promises—to go camping, fishing, and all the boy-father things. . . . The boys felt his lack of attention keenly.

"He's Always Hassled"

Continually harassed, frustrated, worried about finances.

"I'm Never Myself"

Not being able to react to any situation in an *honest* way made it difficult.

I resented having to show up in church every Sunday complete with baby and three kids whether I or they felt like it or not, to listen to the same sermon I'd spent Saturday evening listening to—after turning down invitations for the evening out. . . .

My minister–fiance said I need never take part in the church or play the minister's wife bit. When engaged, I *believed* this nonsense.

"I'm Always Different"

It is troublesome for a minister's wife to be set apart in an intangible way from others in the church. She is set apart because she can have no one as her confidant except her husband. She must often suffer fools, if not gladly, at least patiently, and must reserve personal comments for her husband's ears alone. (But perhaps, if this can be seen positively, it is good discipline.)

"The Parsonage—Wow!"

The house is always someone else's and it's always in a neighborhood a little higher in the social level than you are.

How can one keep a Victorian ark clean and tidy? Getting things fixed at the rectory is a Federal project.

"Money!"

What I'm bitter about is the low salary. He makes less now, after three *more* years of graduate school, than he did before!

I wanted an education, too, but there was no money.

We had no money for counsel when we needed it.

Parson plus matrimony equals parsimony!

Of the common complaint that the ministry is relentless in its demands, there can be no doubt. On this point, however, one study found a surprising number of men, now divorced, who admitted that they had used the "demands of the parish" as an excuse to escape from a dull or problem marriage.

But there are also typical joys. When given a chance, few wives would fail to express themselves vigorously as to the "pro" side of the profession.

Married, or divorced, still "in" or "out," wives often give voice to such opinions as the following:

"I Like Being Special!"

I admit to enjoying the status.

Being part of the limelight and action made me feel important.

I liked having that very special status in the community.

"I Love Meeting People"

It gave me the opportunity to work with and meet all kinds of people I might not otherwise have met.

It brought our family into a whole bright variety of people, situations, and experiences which often have been uniquely the result of his being a minister.

"It's Really a Great Big Family!"

Warm relations with people in the church.

The warmth and interest shown in our children was very beneficial when the children were very young.

I liked being one of the "parents" of our "church family."

"Working With Him"

How many wives *really* know what their husbands do?

"It's Important Work!"

Immensely gratifying to be married to someone
who can understand and share to some extent,
besides feeling that what he is doing is
tremendously important.

Many are happy. Many are ambivalent. All are individuals. The greatest delights for some, pouring tea at recep-
tions, dishing out tons of spaghetti, greeting people after
service, are the bane of others. Some find work in the church
office, grinding away at the old mimeo machine, "meat and
drink." Others keep as far from that mill as they can.

Some say that being a minister's wife rules out an
independent career. Others claim that an outside career is
their formula for maintaining themselves as persons and
wives. Whatever their "formula" or their stance, almost all
clergy wives agree that the price of their very special opportunities is special demands, with built-in tensions and
threats.

There is a powerful, and reciprocal, relationship between ministerial marriage and career. Few who have been
through divorce would put the whole blame on the pastorate: "We would have broken up anyway." But it is an enormous complication and an added strain: "Moving out saved
my marriage!" In short, ministry can be tough on marriage,
and marriage on ministry. "There is something to be said for
celibacy!" as more than one Protestant clergyman has discovered.

No Place to Go

When ministers and their families are in trouble, any
kind of trouble, there is usually no place to go, since letting
one's hair down may mean professional suicide:

When one tells his troubles to his denominational executive, it's a black mark on the Headquarters blotter.

In a small town (another investigator learned) if a clergyman goes to a psychiatrist, his days as a clergyman may be numbered.

There is no place to go where there is genuine concern. "Our denomination," said a wife, "needs a person or persons who can be concerned about the *minister and his family, rather than the church*." Most officials put the welfare of the church and the denomination first. "Our district officer told me," a minister recalled bitterly, "We can always get a new minister, but we can't get a new congregation!"

There is no place to go for specialized understanding and knowledge of clergy problems. "It takes a particular kind of counselor," a clergy wife noted, "to understand a minister's peculiar kind of problems!" There's no place to go where there is an always available, dependable resource. "Every minister needs a minister," said a questionnaire respondent, "and so does his wife."

Up by the Bootstraps. What can be done about it, besides more understanding from parishioners, more consideration from church boards, better pay, and better working and living conditions?

Some clergy wives are discovering they can help themselves. An Episcopal rector's wife tells of a group of wives who met in a therapy project with a psychiatrist, sharing their distress over their situations and problems as ministers' wives. Two were so disturbed they felt ready for individual treatment.

After they had been meeting for a few weeks, the psychiatrist told them: "There's nothing wrong with you that you can't take care of yourselves." So, for ten weeks thereafter they met without him, to share what was uppermost on their minds. Sometimes, things were general and removed from the world of the parish, beliefs, and philosophy, such as, How do you feel about death? When the ten weeks were over, they felt quite good. The two most troubled ones decided that they did not need a psychiatrist, but rather, "we needed each other."

When wives get together, they have some of the same prima donna problems as their husbands. After all, each of them identifies with him fiercely, and her husband is the rival of theirs. The wife is in a further bind, because in most cases it was *he* who chose the career, and she was brought along: happily in some cases, kicking and screaming in others. No matter how happy she may be, there is almost inevitably some adjustment. She is beginning to learn, though, that her greatest allies are other parsons' wives. And in this, she may be learning faster than her man. There are many indications that the wives are turning a corner in sharing the good and the bad. They are beginning to have new kinds of meetings, some with help from experts in human potential, such as encounter trainers and facilitators. After a two-day gathering of wives in Chicago, one said, "It was therapy for me. I am no longer *alone* in that screwy old parsonage. I'm in it with lots of others." Said another: "I've never before been to a wives' meeting where people *really* said what they were thinking."

Even their newsletters have begun to turn corners. Instead of reports of the teas where they "poured," they are beginning to get out their gripes on paper. From a solidly "in" wife:

Letters in the last newsletter from divorced wives
of ministers struck a responsive chord in me. But
for the grace of God, I might have also gone that

way. As a minister's wife I found myself suddenly married into several almost insurmountable situations. One of them is that most of us wives have held good jobs before marriage, only to discover that the church has hired two professional people for less than the price of one.

One of the worst situations is having to find new ways of expressing oneself. A good wife, in most cases, finds devious ways, basking in the glow of his successes, although sometimes pricking the inflated balloon of his ego, and bolstering his spirits in loyalty after his failures. It is not easy to become completely involved in the life of a church but work in the background, never becoming too prominent, especially on controversial issues; to try to be intelligent (for a dumb wife is a great cross to a minister) but never *quite* as intelligent as he.

Wrote another: "Our denomination must face up to the problem of who ministers to ministers' wives."

She begins to find herself, then, as a person not as a shadow. In the discussion group reported by the rector's wife, one wife at last felt free to change her hair color and style of dress every month. They supported and encouraged her in what her parish saw as eccentricity. "Don't apologize," they told her. "This is what makes you *you!*"

Happily Ever After

There is a happy side to the turbulence in the parsonage, even to departures and divorce. Some of the traumas have made the clergy more "human" and helped their people see them as "normal." Says one man: "It's lonely as hell, of course, but one thing: my divorce has made me more human, more understanding. More people come to me for counsel than before."

Clergy couples are refusing, more and more, to put up with dull, meaningless marriages, drab, make-do arrangements. They are finding the courage to close out bad situations. The divorces and departures don't have to be read as a sign of moral collapse. Quite the opposite: they are much more a sign that people now expect more of themselves, of one another, more of their marriages than ever before. A divorced minister writes: "Personal fulfillment has become a valid goal. Career is less important. You can even choose both, today."

Research brings us yet another clue here. These divorced clergy marry, the next time around, not the red-headed chorus girl or the leggy model, but someone with whom they can be more completely themselves, and build a three dimensional life. More than one who has "run off with the education director" has thereby hooked up with a partner who can share more than the diurnal doings of the parsonage: the developments and meanings of the job, in larger dimensions.

One study turned up two cases of ministers remarrying the person he had divorced. But this time it was different: A former ex-wife said: "The divorce literally helped us both see our true images and realize we weren't as 'bad,' or expected to be as 'perfect,' as we thought. A tremendous amount of maturity resulted from our being separated. I found a new kind of love with my husband." The quest of these seeking and storm-tossed clergy is the same quest of the marrying priests: to be more a person, and to be more richly fulfilled.

CHAPTER SEVEN

The Case of the Vanishing Parson

One thing can be said: the parson is a remarkable person. He is superior, in intelligence, in talent, in potential. He is superior also, in perceptivity and dedication. These are the views of Thomas E. Brown, Director of the Northeast Career Center, whose clergy counseling agency at Princeton, New Jersey, has tested and conferred with more than eight hundred clergymen since its inception. Most of these clients are from the three member denominations: Presbyterian, Episcopal, and Lutheran. Though this sample may be "a cut above ministers generally," he says of them unequivocally, "they are in the upper intellectual bracket, the top one to five percent of the population. On our rating scales, they score 'superior' or 'very superior.' "

Brown concludes, "The unfortunate and disappointing thing, however, is that the minister does not even *begin* to realize his potential."

Since his field is people, and his concern is with meaning, the pastor can't help looking at himself and the meanings of his own life work. In the words of two men

who have analyzed some seven hundred psychological studies of clergymen, Robert J. Menges and James E. Dittes, the
effectiveness or adequacy of past performance is in his case
"necessarily subject to excruciatingly personal appraisal."
Thus, introspectiveness and self-analysis are built into the
"clerical profile."

Put them together: his high potential, high sensitivity, and high hopes on the one hand, with the low visible
result of his labors, his sense of ineffectiveness and futility in
his present setting, on the other, and no wonder the clergyman is restless! If he is not fully aware of his superior capabilities he *is* aware of what needs doing. The discrepancy
between what "is" and "ought to be," or more important,
what *could* be—is the gap which frustrates and maddens him.

Stained Glass Cage

Whatever he is doing to block his own fulfillment,
blocking him also are other forces quite outside and beyond
his control. Two of these "other forces" he perceives as
boxes or cages, which fence in his creativity.

Cage 1 is the church itself: its rigidity and what he
sees as its unresponsiveness to the human condition and the
cries of its own people. It is not just its concrete enclosure of
doctrine and ritual and formal expectation, but its prescribed
pattern of behavior and human relationships. The shape of
the box may vary, from the "little brown church in the vale"
to the "more stately mansion" in Megalopolis. But wherever
it is, it binds.

Take "worship" for example, with its prepackaged
order of service, its bits and pieces, its equal time for credits,
solicitations, and commercials. Take that letter from the
bishop: "We're moving you to Keokuk." *Just* as he was
getting something going in Dubuque! Or that warning not

to push that petition, and to lay off a bit on talking about the war.

It's not that the parson wants or expects total freedom. Far from it. He, like his brother clergyman, is generally accepting of, even dependent on, structure. Tests show that he may want independence while *being* dependent. After all, he has been schooled in letting the structure run him, rather than his running it.

What he did not know was how scared they'd be, how resistant to change, how unwilling to move when moving was called for. He was quite unprepared for that institution–reflex, that automatic stiffening of the joints in response to a suggestion of something new. He had no idea how these fine, smiling parishioners would literally stiffen into a "board" when they became trustees. What got into them? What happened, for that matter, to his erstwhile fellow-crusader, good old Sam, when he became a bishop? Is no one committed to the vital religion he says he wants?

Cage 2 is the image of "clergyman" itself. This is more subtle than the carefully articulated patterns of authority, but quite as potent: that creepy, silent ministerial stereotype. It is like a cobweb brushed across his face: he can wipe and grope and pick at it but he can never quite find it and it won't go away.

That phony deference, for instance: the quick cover-up of the paperback sex book on the subway. Or the damper-on-the-party feeling: the noise suddenly stops when he comes in the room (like one of the old Dracula movies: when the monster is loose the crickets quit singing). It's those stupid–sad little jokes: sentencing the parrot to the basement when the preacher comes to dinner.

The clerical image is always there, whispering what a minister should be like. How he should walk and talk and dress and look. What he should and should not do—especially what he should not do.

A Methodist preacher has captured the stereotype for them all, in *How to Become a Bishop Without Being Religious*. Says Charles Merrill Smith:

> Now you may have a taste for shaggy sport coats, gay ties, livid hosiery and the like. If so, you must ruthlessly suppress it. Such apparel is associated, in the minds of the good people you will serve with flamboyance, worldliness and instability. Who would turn for spiritual counsel to a man in a tweed sport coat?

> Another . . . index to a man's personality is his motorcar. Psychological research tells us that we reveal a great deal about our inner selves by our choice of an automobile. It is at the same time a sign of our station in society, a way of expressing our hidden frustrations and subconscious, longings, and, incidentally, a means of transportation.

> Now to a pastor, a car is absolutely essential. Of necessity he will spend a great many hours in it. It represents the largest single item in his budget after food. The selection of the 'right' car, therefore, deserves considerable attention.

After discussing the various colors and makes of vehicles, with their corresponding symbolism, Smith says: ". . . we arrive at a black standard two-door Falcon sedan as the ideal automobile for the beginning clergyman." Smith continues:

> Everybody has his own little peculiarities, ways of doing things, characteristic facial expressions, reactions to others, moods, affectations, etc., which

we lump under the heading of personal habits and which total up to our public personality.

It is absolutely essential to the preacher's image that he hedge in his natural inclinations with a rugged set of custom-made inhibitions.

It is essential . . . to project a mild but distinct quality of asceticism. . . . A prudent preacher . . . will never use alcohol or tobacco. . . . He will never, never tell an off-color story, and when one is told in his presence he will react with a slight frown followed by a very brief, tolerant, superior smile which will make the teller feel sinful and embarrassed.

Your congregation, although it does not understand this, pays you to be good for them. . . . You are, in a very real sense, the modern Protestant equivalent of the ancient Jewish scapegoat upon which the sins of the people were heaped and thus expiated.

A preacher who appears to be getting a lot of fun out of life does not impress the laity as a very good scapegoat.

Clergy researchers found this bestselling caricature remarkably accurate. Sociology professors assign it to their students. The public found it hilarious and responded by pushing it up the ladder of most-read books. But for the clergyman "it ain't funny."

Morality, Inc.

In Smith's book, and elsewhere, there is more substance than a few mild and stale jokes at the parson's expense.

Here, rather, is the symptom and symbol of the degeneration of morality into petty *moralism*.

In his concentrated, localized, and denatured goodness, Parson Jones serves to relieve his constituency of the necessity of being good. He is good for them, their walking surrogate conscience and model. He is a device by which society also makes religion irrelevant, reducing it to triviality. The labels for the symbolic Parson Jones are no accident. He is "preacher" (who preaches at you), or "pastor" (I am your shepherd and you are a silly sheep), or "minister" (who does good unto you). "Rabbi" at least has the advantage of meaning teacher and custodian of tradition. (But, even this is a reproach to any Jew at war with Jewishness!) Finally, we have "rector" (who corrects you). The professional religious stereotype is thus so rooted in being *judgmental* that it would be very difficult to change. Black suit and stiff collar do not help.

The stereotype makes him something less than human. He's caught in a double bind. If he buys this image, he becomes a buffoon, whose real message can be ignored. If he rejects it, he's a man without a role. Understandably, the boxed-in parson feels a mighty urge to break out. The really remarkable thing may not be "how many are leaving," but how many are staying.

First Presbyterian Self

One of the things that shows up in the minister's three-day stay at the Princeton center (where his career is tested, weighed and measured, stabbed and sliced), is the extent to which Joe Pastor draws his very identity from the organization that hires him, rather than from his profession or himself.

As one ex-nun said of her former existence: "You're not yourself, you're the Order—you're the Sacred Heart

Convent. You're what it stands for and all it should mean in the outside world." But she's better off than the minister, in that she understands this. She took the vow of obedience, intentionally subordinating her own self and will. He doesn't see it, doesn't know that he has no self but the First Presbyterian Me.

Part of the resulting trauma is that anything that goes wrong in the church is somehow his doing. Church spats are intensely personal; church splits, almost fatal. He sees such things not as normal group behavior, challenges in conflict management, but as blameworthy disasters that may finish him.

So, in another important sense, the parson *is* vanishing. As an ecclesiastical organization man, his person has been transmogrified into a Parson. Yet originally, and literally as Webster defines it, "parson" means "person," *the* person in the community. As Chaucer wrote: "the povre Persoun, the good man of religion, that first wroghte and afterward he taughte." To restore to him today some of "self," it is necessary to remove several layers of institutional siding. Thomas E. Brown says:

> My main job is to help people see that *they're* the key, not the church. I want to give them some calcium in their backbones, some sense of *personal* and *professional* identity, so they can stand or fall on their own, regardless of what happens in the church. When you have an ambivalent organization —which most churches are—*and* an ambivalent leader, you have a mess!

Beyond knowing where he wants to go, the parson needs something more: the techniques of how to get there, how to get results. These, the seminary does not teach. If he wants change, he must become a change agent. His idea of changing people now is to preach at them. He must learn how to move people, how to make something happen, how to use conflict. Now, he fights his institution, fights his people. It uses *him*.

The most significant statistic at the Center may be that, though most of its clients are disturbed, distressed or frustrated in their work, fewer than twenty percent move out of the church after they go through this rethinking process.

"Dropout" Is a Dirty Word

As researchers dig into the "dropout" phenomenon, one startling finding keeps coming to light: hundreds upon hundreds who have left do not feel, in their own minds, that they have left at all.

In a report on clergy who have left the United Church of Christ, Edgar Mills states (1970) "The ex-pastors certainly don't consider themselves as having 'left the ministry.' Only 13.9% of them would accept such a description." Sixty-two percent of those called "ex-pastors" in this study see themselves as performing a ministry in their current jobs.

"We didn't leave the ministry," explained a United Church man in Chicago. "The ministry left us."

Mills agrees: "Ex-pastors," he says, "but—with few exceptions—not ex-ministers."

Another investigation, looking into what it called "displaced" Episcopal clergy, brought some irate replies: From a teacher:

> I do not consider that I am 'displaced.' . . . Such terms as 'have left,' 'decided to leave' . . . seem to me to be reflecting a personal attitude that I frankly do not share.

From a Peace Corps administrator in Tanzania:

Having recently digested the collected essays of
Thomas J. J. Altizer and William Hamilton,
which together with Harvey Cox, makes me
wonder whether I am *that* 'displaced.'

From the headmaster of a parochial school:

> I have always been associated with . . . ministry.
> Unfortunately, the Church Annual happily listed
> me in the nonparochial section for reasons all their
> own.

Some clergymen, the report concluded, though classified by the church as nonparochial, feel themselves to be
"more parochial" than the urban rector.

A report on Unitarian Universalist ministers shifting
out of the parish ministry states that "almost all of those who
have shifted to nonparish work declare that they are *ministers still:* some in a broad and general sense, others, quite
specifically."

Some sample comments about their career shifts:

- Do you mean to tell me that teaching courses in
  religion to hundreds of students is not a ministry
  in the full sense?

- My present work for this agency on mental re-
  tardation is *more* of a ministry than much of the
  parish work I've done . . . without all the hassle
  of disgruntled neurotic parishioners and trustees!

- Working toward my doctorate in adult education
  is much better than the parish . . . if there is anything churchianity is unprepared to cope with, it's
  religion. Ministry in the sense of relating to the
  real religious concern which is not only outside

'church' but anti-'church.' I'm glad you specify 'parish' ministry, because I don't think I'll ever leave the ministry broadly construed, let alone return to it.

One can understand from these responses why "dropout" is a dirty word.

The Parish Hangup

A great many who have left are not angry at anyone, not even the church. But they are angry at something else: the nonparish stigma. For almost everyone, in churches and out, the parish ministry is regarded as *the* ministry. The minute preachers cease to be candidates for parish jobs, headquarters loses interest. The minute they are out of the pulpit, they are out of the public eye and forgotten.

An Episcopal seminary professor, Helon Chichester, says:

> In popular conversation with laymen . . . I have found that *without exception* ordination is associated with the parochial ministry. Parish ministers are for the most part the only kind a layman ever sees, and therefore, the parochial ministry is 'The Ministry.'

This interpretation by laity is quite in line with official interpretations. The publication *Theological Education* noted not long ago that "Protestant doctrines of ministry have tended to confine the ordained ministry rigidly to the local church." (The Roman Catholic tradition gives greater recognition to other ministries.) As a consequence, Protestants depreciate ministries not directly connected with the local congregation. Chichester goes further, reporting "feelings of hostility" toward those who elected to leave the parish.

This sentiment is more than sentiment alone. In some denominations the move to a nonparish ministry means automatic change of status. Lutherans have such a category, known as "awaiting a call." (Don't wait too long: three years is "out"!) When ministers move to less than half-time on the church payroll, Unitarian Universalists transfer them from "full" to "associate" status.

More annoying than official demotion, however, is the psychological demotion. A district executive of one large denomination, otherwise happy enough, complains bitterly: "Again and again I meet with former parishioners, who say: 'I didn't know you'd left the ministry.'"

The Larger Parish

In any case, uncounted numbers of "ex" or "displaced" or "shifted" ministers feel they are ministers still. In spite of these traumas, when they do get their bearings, they may wish that they had made the move much sooner. For, as the Unitarian Universalist study reports, "By and large those who have shifted say they are happier and better off in work, backing, pay, and prospects than they were as parish ministers."

As one of its respondents, a junior college teacher, said:

> What I was trying to do for youth in my parish shook people up too much. Here, they are serious about helping youth, as persons and in terms of giving them new skills. . . . Unlike my church, they pay me to deepen my competence . . . my salary is a couple of thousand above what my church provided.

United Church ex-pastors earn more, are freer and more relaxed, and report improved financial and family situations. Only one in ten replying said things had not improved. The others listed their gains as follows:

- twenty-one percent say working conditions are better; more money, more security, more time, better housing.

- twenty-nine percent say personal factors are better: less tense, happier.

- twenty-eight percent say the new job is more satisfying, more fulfilling (uses more skills).

- fourteen percent say they are "more human," that is, they "relate to people more realistically."

Lest all this sound too euphoric, it must be added that many who have attained this vantage point have done so at great personal sacrifice. Many pay the price for their shift by giving up retirement benefits, security, and tenure. Most also relinquish familiar surroundings, friends, and colleagues. These, of course, on top of the frightening plunge into a world of jobs that is new and strange.

An editorial writer says "I miss the contacts with people." A former priest, who was also a college dean, confesses, "Punching a time clock and being checked on by a petty young upstart takes some getting used to. It's demeaning."

A man now managing a string of apartments says "my present work is just that—*work*. I do not like it. I was angry at myself for failing to bring off my retirement smoothly, but utterly relieved to be out of our spiritual kindergarten. I will get out of this present work in a few years when my estate is sufficient to keep me."

There are often years of treading water: "Fortunately I inherited a small estate. This tided me over until at last I realized the ministry was not for me. I'm selling insurance now. It's hard going. If this doesn't work I'll just try something else." Another says: "Maybe the ministry exists to provide people who will work for low wages for good causes like the one I'm in. My wife got a job as clerk–typist. We manage but we're still in debt."

Many are still floundering.

Three Who Vanished

The following are three cases of parsons who "vanished." Their names are real. Their stories are true. They are, and have been, ministers. They are not cited here as "typical" cases—none is typical—but rather, as victims of typical failings in church systems, whose narrow, conventional categories cannot accept them as ministers in the full sense.

Case 1 is the story of a man and his equally dedicated wife, who brought compassion, sensitivity, talent, and commitment to the ministry. Their church did not reject them. It just was not aware that they were there. Except for a nameless clerk who belatedly sent them a bill for health insurance, it took no notice when they left.

Case 2 is a man with more expertise than his church could utilize. He was what agencies call "overqualified." *He* had to figure out how to package his services to the church, and the package would not fit the church's bins.

Case 3 is a man who knew and from the beginning pursued his calling in a firm, straight line. He never wavered, but the church routings never fitted him. On his journey, every time he crossed a county line, they felt he needed a new visa. In the end he didn't leave: they classified him "out"!

Joe Schneiders is self-educated. He went to high

school at night while battling his way, daytime, as a factory worker in Detroit's lean and bloody Thirties. Later he did well in radio, drama, public relations work. As a layman he was "turned on" by the liberal social sentiments of a local minister and decided to become a minister himself.

Schneiders' personal motto, he says, is a phrase of Norman Cousins: "a blazing sense of restlessness to set things right." The church was to be his vehicle. That was what it proclaimed itself, in the press releases Joe's practiced eye picked up.

Too poor to go to seminary, he was permitted to study a syllabus. From the church's point of view this was a concession, but for him it was a humiliating bore: "It consisted of being able to talk about theologians meeting in 1880, a lot of dry church history and so on. People kept putting me down because I'd had no formal education. What made it extra tough was, I had no great respect for these 'intellectual powers' who were putting me down." Finally he made it, and started up the parish ladder. The staid little churches he was assigned were emphatically not ready for a parson who acted on his social convictions, though he says "There wasn't a thing we were pushing that the denomination hadn't passed resolutions about every time they had a convention!"

Schneiders' style was startling then, though since it has begun to be accepted. Said he:

> I'd had twenty years supporting myself in public relations. I can write. I can do sermons. But I just think that the verbal doesn't make it.
>
> That is why, instead of preaching, I simply threw out ideas—and more than that, I brought in, for example, Aid to Dependent Mothers women and let them talk; an ex-drug addict youth and let him

talk. My role was just to point things up. I felt a
real 'religious experience' might come in people's
response to what they got, this way, first hand.

But they didn't like some of the people who came.
One pillar of the church said 'Some of those young
ladies are not wearing *hose!*' Actually they were
Notre Dame students and their friends. Of course,
none of them had any money, so I wasn't
attracting the kind of folks who would pay our
bills.

The people cut their pledges and Joe's wife, Lynn,
had to get a job. She is qualified both as a teacher and social
worker but "our work for civil rights made us 'hot.' " So
she had to go into the next state to get work."

The denouement came when backlash rightists set
the church afire. "I called up headquarters," Joe recalled,

because I didn't know what to do when your
church gets burned. Also, I needed some solid
backing: people were saying I was a communist or
something.

The trouble was, it was summertime, and when I
finally reached somebody I was told 'It's vacation
time! Too bad.' Months later some of my minister
brothers sent sympathies but it was too late. What
I got from the church, even from my local church
board, was *just plain silence*. And the reaction:
'See what you've done. It's really not very nice to
get our church burned.'

"Disenchantment" is the word that sums it up for
the Schneiders. "We bought it as a package. We really gave
ourselves to it. Now, it's like a dream we'd like to forget."

Some bitterness they admit to, but Joe says: "I am not trying to judge my colleagues. I'm just saying that, as I see what they're doing, this is not something I wish to spend my life at."

Today he's working—with a couple of dozen other ex-clergy—for the Michigan Civil Rights Commission—in public relations, his original forte. Lynn is working too, one of a special corps whose task is to prepare the people in various strife-torn neighborhoods to take control of their own public schools.

"Put me down this way," was his parting word, "I'm not disillusioned with *religion*, just with the institutional church."

Rev. Theodore R. Smith, founder–member of the American Association of Pastoral Counselors, can be described either as counselor or as minister, and is quite consciously both. "I began life as an engineer," he relates, "and then discovered religious people and then I discovered people, then I became concerned with the question: What is human nature? And here I am."

Smith has established an independent practice in New York, but he has affiliations, on the one hand with colleagues in the counseling field per se, and on the other, with churches. In fact he has an office in a church on the West Side, with part time office hours, and is accepted as a referral resource by the local ministers' association to which he belongs. He is not, however, on any church's payroll; indeed he feels his value to the church is partly that he stands on his own feet as an accredited professional in his own field of counseling.

Smith feels that all that he does is "ministry," but his application for regular ministerial status, again, has caused bureaucrats headaches. Ironically, he may well turn out to be not simply a "minister" but a theologian: since his practice and study are focused on theological issues in contemporary psychology, for example, whether Freudian analysis is too deterministic. But his resolution of this question will, in all likelihood, come from observation of fellow humans rather than scripture!

Gene R. Reeves, a professor at Wilberforce University in Ohio, illustrates the lameness of bureaucratized attempts to make do with a narrow "parish" definition of ministry. Dr. Reeves' basic career choice occurred when he was a college sophomore and "has never changed." His aim was the teaching of meaning—either as a college teacher, or maybe as a minister. He had no church tie: religion for him never was identified with a particular church; in fact when he felt he ought to join one, he picked what seemed "the best of a bad lot." But while working toward his doctorate, he says,

> I came to respect many of the guys I was in school with, many of the clergy I met, and many of the churches I attended. I developed an enormous respect for the potential importance of religious institutions . . . I came to think of the parish ministry as a viable option for me . . . [though] it never supplanted teaching as my first choice.

> Toward the end of my time at Boston University, I approached the Department of Ministry about certification as a minister. Since *parish* ministry was not my aim . . . [the executive] . . . was against it and even attempted to talk me out of applying. . . . I persisted.

While completing his doctorate, however, Reeves became so involved with the parish as to fill in for a pastor on leave. "So I was ordained."

That made him O.K. in the eyes of Headquarters.

He was a full-status minister. He remained so when he presently accepted a teaching post—because it happened to be in
one of the denomination's own seminaries. Then, he moved
from the seminary to a position at Wilberforce, attracted
there in part by the chance to share his knowledge with
black university students. The denomination automatically
moved him out of full status although, he explained, "I don't
feel any more or less a minister."

He concludes:

> There is a general point I would like to make. We
> don't think it strange for people other than clergy
> to have more than one vocational option. . . . But
> our attitude toward clergy is . . . that . . . the
> ministry has to be the only thing he wants to
> do. . . . I know I am not the only one with quite
> positive attitudes toward *parish* ministry, for
> whom it is nevertheless not the only thing I would
> like to do.

In sum: what many of these relocated ministers are
saying is that far from dropping out: they are dropping *in* to
new spheres, new contexts, and new relations where they
are, at last, free to minister. They find that they do not need
the label "denominationally approved," like "government-
inspected beef," as long as they can be effective as persons
and parsons.

In this fluid and changing time, it would be impossible to say who or what the "new parson" will be. We only
know that he is finding new slots, new ways, new forms.
There are many who would join with the ex-clergyman who
declared "I'm more of a minister *now* than I ever was. I'm
more of a person, too." Some would even agree no doubt,
with the rabbi who left his temple under a cloud, but now
exclaims, "I lost Culver City, but I gained the world."

CHAPTER EIGHT

The called
and the calling

"There's no two ways about it! Ministers are mama's boys!" This was the declaration of a seminary student in early 1970, at a conference of seminarians and clergy in Cambridge, Massachusetts. It wasn't a top-of-the-head remark.

> What I'm saying I really know about. I've been researching the subject for twenty-five years. I'm a P.K.—a preacher's kid, or if you prefer, a clergy brat. And I can tell you from experience, that when I was growing up, I would have settled for *anything* else when they asked me what my father did. Something male and strong and easy to explain, like 'fixing pipes' or 'repairing wires' or 'hammering boards.'

In a search for clues to the state of clergy restlessness, William Easter, designer of the Resources Center for Parish Clergy in Lubbock, Texas, interviewed some six hundred persons across the country: ex-clergy and those who work with them. On the basis of his many interviews, he concluded that the ministry attracts "mainly feminine types." He found most clergy to be "lacking in male aggressiveness" and "in want of mothering." He also confirmed the findings of a counseling specialist who observed that clergy tend to come from a prototype background: strong ties with the mother and rejection by the father.

The pattern is this: Junior goes to seminary. Father always "knew there was something wrong" but Mother is thrilled. He remembers Father as oppressive, but Mother was "the Virgin Mary on wheels." The result: considerably less than a full-grown man.

If these observations are correct, one may ask: Is there a ministerial type? Solid research in this area is limited, but from those who test and counsel and work with them, the word comes through: Yes, *the minister is a type.*

Parson's Profile

There are exceptions of course, and any "clergy traits" are unevenly distributed through the different denominations and across the board. But from returns now in, the profile begins to look like this:

Ministers tend to be *dependent.* They may rail at the church and its requirements; they may resent its restrictions, they may even leave in desperation, but they enjoy its protection, and want to be cared for. They began their ministry by being "called" and have been conditioned and confirmed in a "holding pattern" ever since: "awaiting a call" from a different parish, or waiting for a raise, or for repairs to the leaking parsonage roof.

Closely allied with dependence is *passivity* and a "hesitancy in promoting oneself," reinforced by the fact that, as one Episcopal bishop remarked, "it is bad form to seek advancement." Passivity does not refer to a clergyman's *movements*—he may be hyperactive—but to his level of decision and decisiveness.

From his work with Lutheran clergy, Albert Haversat concludes that

> The major ministerial crisis is self-image, that is,
> dependency and lack of confidence. He may bitch
> about 'church structure'—but this only helps him
> to avoid facing *himself*.

> The ministry attracts dependent and permissive
> types. 'Dependent' in that he needs someone to
> take care of him and build him up, 'permissive' in
> that he has a low ability to *decide* and *confront*.
> He is afraid of conflict, and so relies on avoidance.

Part of the dependency complex is the "feminine" component, referred to above. "Money and power are male symbols," says one observer, "and the clergy have trouble with them *both*."

Tests run at the Princeton clergy counseling center show that at least half of their clients are introverted. There is nothing wrong with introverts. However, as the director there notes:

> Running a voluntary association in an activist age
> takes a sure hand on the wheel. All too many
> clergymen, we find, lack the requisite firmness and
> active assurance that their positions call for. Not
> only does this lack produce a conflict between him
> and the institution, but also within himself. There
> is a built-in tension in leading a voluntary
> institution, if the leader is an introvert.

Clergy are encouraged to bring their wives to participate in the program at this Northeast Career Center, and forty percent have done so. They are often more candid than the men. Many are distressed that their husbands are so weak and wavering. "When he asks me how shall he handle a board or congregational problem, what shall I tell him? If *he* doesn't know what to do, how should I? *He's* the minister!"

In one wife's words: "I'd not mind disagreeing with him, or feeling that he's wrong. If he'd only *take a stand!*"

Parson's Paradox. One intriguing aspect of the clergyman's profile is a peculiar contradiction—an inward indecision combined with and cloaked in an external aggressiveness. This outward sound and fury conceal an inner marshmallow. It has taken a long time to discover this softness underneath, because the camouflage is so thick, *viz.:*

- from his incomparable pulpit eminence the parson has been permitted—no, required—to sound off. And he does.
- with his diffuse mishmash of roles: marry and bury, symbolize and sanction, anoint and bless, he's all over the landscape and charging in a dozen different directions.
- he teaches and preaches, writes and speaks, pronounces and comforts, chairs meetings, raises money: a real "takeover guy" one would say.
- his schedule is often frantic, noisy, exhibitionistic,
- while his wife or secretary holds things together.

This schizoid aggressiveness–dependency helps to explain a great many things. His high achievement motivation, for example. He must achieve, and keep achieving, to down his inner doubts.

"The minister is, I suppose," says the Rev. J. A. Crane of Santa Barbara,

in some sense, the servant of God; but at the same
time he is also serving himself, is also satisfying his
own most deeply felt needs . . . he feels good as
he burns himself out for God. He is giving of
himself, yes; but he is also getting what he needs.
He is driven by his performer's needs, by his lust
for widespread approval, to do many good works
in the world, no matter what the cost to himself.

Pouring out his life to the glory of God, and going prayer-
fully to his martyrdom, Dr. Crane submits

is a rather messy kind of masochistic self-
abnegation . . . a grand rationalization which
allows the minister to satisfy his own rather
neurotic need for large-scale approval and
acceptance, while charging it up to the glory of
God.

This surface activism with which he deceives and
soothes himself is both escape and compensation: escape
from the matters he does not know how to handle; compensation for the returns he wants, but does not receive.

More than mere achieving, though, he must see the
results. Here is the greatest frustration for many. It is not
in the nature of parish work to show quick results. Slow ger-
mination may look like failure, so the need for reassurance
mounts. He has to be told again and again that the meeting
"went well"; the program "succeeded"; the canvass "topped
the goal"; the sermon was "the greatest." The suspicion that
others, especially laymen, can do as well as he in some en-
deavors can drive him wild. "When you see what laypeople
can do," one more than usually candid pastor confessed,
"you have the slightly apprehensive feeling that the legend
of clerical indispensability is being challenged."

A clergy counselor says he often hears from clients: "*My* gospel must mean something! If what I say has no more weight than what is said by a layman, I want to get out!"

So the hunger for success can draw him into the trap he preaches against: the numbers game of the "materialistic world": head counts, the "up" line on the graph, angling for "big givers."

The minister is a loner. Any executive or top organization-man is to some extent. But he is the loner supreme, forced into that position by the prevailing stereotype of ministry. It cuts him off from people, and if one accepts its tempting limelight and adulation, will subvert even those whose instincts are healthier. He winds up competing with himself and everybody else for lines, applause, and power.

Researchers complain that too little attention has been given to studying peer-relations among ministers. *What* peer relations? Clergy are, with one another, jealous as siblings, nervous as cats. Multi-ministries tend to be tugs of war; clergy conferences, games of one-upmanship: "More people call me at 3:00 A.M. than call you at 3:00 A.M." Someone should write a book on "Games Clergy Play."

As one young ex-clergyman wrote: "A get-together didn't mean a chance to find a little comfort or understanding . . . instead it meant another round of intellectual games."

A psychiatrist told a ministers' conference not long ago:

> There is some sort of bad relationship built into clergymen's relationships with one another. Do they ever get together to share *failures*, as well as successes? . . . Apparently the price of failure is too high. Even to admit it costs too much.

The United Church of Christ researchers asked this question of pastors and ex-pastors:

Most of us appreciate receiving praise for work well done. During your pastorate, please indicate how much you would have valued the praise of each of the persons or groups listed below:

1. Fellow pastors of the same denomination.
2. Denominational executives who know your work.
3. Lay leaders in congregation.
4. Wife or husband.
5. Fellow pastors in churches of same community.
6. Others on your church staff (if any).
7. Close friends not included above.

Respondents, both those still "in" and those who had moved "out," demoted fellow-clergy to the bottom of the list.

Their ratings:

Ex-pastors	Pastors
Wife	Wife
Close friends	Lay leaders
Lay leaders	Close friends
Denominational executive	Others on church staff
Others on church staff	Denominational executive
Fellow UCC pastors	Fellow UCC pastors
Other pastors in community	Other pastors in community

Other Side of the Coin. If these are his "problem" traits, they are, of course, combined with and outweighed by his many remarkable strengths and positive qualities discussed above: his deep caring and commitment which attracted him to the ministry, his unusual sensitivity, creativity, his superior intelligence. Psychological tests also show that, as with lawyers, authors, and journalists, persons attracted to the ministry tend to be unusually gifted in ability to organize materials and ideas.

The strongest interests and aptitudes of clergy, reflected clearly in tests and reinforced by their own statements and behavior, are, like those of teachers, social workers, and public administrators, almost inevitably centered around people.

In view of his person-centered inclinations, one cannot help wondering how he so often relates to parishioners by an unhealthy upstage pattern, and to his brother ministers by putting them down. Part of it doubtless has to do with his "need to be needed" disposition, the dependency beneath the aggressiveness. But even more may be due to a neurosis of the institution itself and its clergy stereotype, which gets in the way of genuine caring and community.

The "X" in Exodus

As the clergy exodus mounts, more and more people are trying to locate that unknown quantity, that mysterious, missing "x" which separates those who leave the parish (Species A) from those who stay in it (Species B). No one has found it yet, for at least two reasons: 1) the line between the two will not stay put, and 2) there are too many factors involved.

As for the first, a goodly portion of those staying are like ripe plums, inwardly ready to drop off the tree. One survey, of three thousand Protestant clergy, reported that two-thirds of the entire sample had at some time contemplated leaving their parishes. Another cross-denominational study found that thirty percent of the sample were seriously considering leaving at the time they were questioned. Reports just released on clergy of a major denomination reveal that at present two-thirds of them would opt for a change of some sort: forty-seven percent have thought of, or are thinking of, leaving the parochial ministry, and twenty-one percent, of leaving the ministry altogether.

As for the second, there being too many factors, a 1965 survey of United Presbyterian ex-clergy dredged up no less than twenty-five different factors which had influenced decisions to leave, ranging from job satisfaction to health. Edgar Mills, who conducted the study, has since remarked that human decisions are "over-determined," that is, a single incident may tip the scale, but "a life-decision is never the result of just one influence." When ex-pastors of another denomination were asked, "What was your main reason for leaving the parish?" no single reason received a "high" rating from as many as half of the respondents.

Always, people are changing careers, sometimes voluntarily, sometimes against their will—for poor health, both mental and physical, for incompetence, for personality reasons. The church is no exception; but one would expect there to be something different or special about it. Researchers keep looking for the key. So far, as possible clues, they have looked at such items as money, age, mobility, education, and special training.

Money. Clergy pay may be disgraceful: about factory-worker level, but very few leave for reasons of money alone.

Age and length of service in the ministry. Some defections may be traced to impatient youth, but most who leave do so much nearer mid-career. Nearly two-thirds of the United Church of Christ ex-pastors left *after* the age of thirty-five. American Baptists leave at average age forty. Lutheran Church of America and United Presbyterian figures are similar.

One vocational counseling firm discovered that its Protestant clients were almost ten years older than its Catholic clients: the average age for priests defecting being thirty-five, and for ministers, forty-four.

Change patterns. Many of those who leave already have a pattern of moving around—in and out of church work, in and out of specific assignments, in and out of denominations, shorter pastorates. Conservative Jews leaving synagogues come to the clergy-help agency, Bearings, Inc., with twenty to thirty previous congregational appointments, as compared, for the same period, with the usual two or three. More of those leaving Unitarian Universalism had transferred earlier from other denominations. More than half of the UCC ex-pastors were "come-outers" also.

Education. Those with more education seem more likely to leave. At least, former Congregational and other UCC ex-pastors have what that report called "substantially" higher education than that of the pastors who remained. In the National Association for Pastoral Renewal (Roman Catholic) with a membership composed both of pastors and ex-pastors, ten percent more of those who have left have higher degrees than have those who stay.

Specialized training. Those with special or additional training, beyond the standard ministerial preparation, seem more likely to leave their church institutions. For example, within Roman Catholicism, more specialized priests depart, than do general parish priests. Ph.D.s—a high proportion among Reform Jews and Jesuits—can and do transfer easily to university and college teaching.

A somewhat sad commentary: clergymen who acquire supplementary skill in order to have a more effective ministry, are then often lost to the church. Outside agencies lure them away because they can pay them better and use them better.

In the early days of the present wave of clergy defection, those leaving were shrugged off as "misfits" and "malcontents." Now many who deal with them feel that it may be the most qualified who are leaving. To quote from one report:

> A frequent and convenient excuse for ignoring the challenge of career shifts is to say that 'the man who doesn't make it in the ministry just doesn't have it.' It is evident, from the jobs they hold, and the money they make, that a great many of those who shift to other careers *do* have it, by almost any standard and in comparison with both their old and their new peers.

> Some . . . go into teaching, and emerge as deans and department heads. Some go into social work, and end by managing the agency.

On October 29, 1969, The *National Catholic Reporter* warned of an impending "brain drain" in the church. It quoted Dean C. Dauw of Human Resource Developers in Chicago as saying that his firm had found jobs recently for former heads of three major seminaries. Cele Caestecker of Next Step observed that her organization had been helping "in the last two years . . . more and more of the creative dynamic kinds of people." Mrs. Patricia Roy, of New York's Bearings remarked that "this year (1969) is the first time we have dealt with chancellors, vicars general, monsignors."

Father Eugene Schallert, research sociologist at the

University of San Francisco, cautions, however, that no adequate comparison has yet been made between those who go and those who stay.

Vital Variable: Self-Image

Almost nothing has been done in the early research, certainly nothing definitive, with the self-image of clergy. The search for the missing "x" goes on, but until we explore this factor adequately, we will not have the picture. Two aspects of self-image are important here: 1) what he identifies with, i.e. his central focus, and 2) his ministerial "style."

The pastor's primary personal identification can be either a *cause*, abetted by his profession, or an *institution*, in this case, the church. The Northeast Career Center discovered that a great many ministers identify first and foremost with the organization: denomination, or parish. It is not that they deny their goals or their profession, but, like the nun in her convent, the fundamental self-image and identity derive from the church.

With the institution as the primary focus, it cannot help but be seen as an end in itself, and something important, per se, to preserve. With institution-centered types, there is a strong urge to stick by the church, come what may. Other factors may win out, of course, but institutional identity is a key factor in his decision. (Eighty percent of Northeast Career Center clients stay in the church.)

For the more cause-centered person, the institution is important, but as a *means*. When the institution ceases to deliver on the cause, he can leave. When the institution stands in his way, he *wants* to leave. The line here is not simply between those *in* the church and those *out*, but between contrasting versions of relating to it, *both* in and out.

At the risk of oversimplification, sample alternatives might look like this:

A.   STAYING IN

1. *Institutional Focus:*
   "No matter what: my church right or wrong"

2. *Cause Focus:*
   "It needs changing and I want to help"

B.   GETTING OUT

1. *Institutional Focus:*
   "Since I'm out, I'll go somewhere else"

2. *Cause Focus:*
   "With the church what it is, I can minister better elsewhere"

A–1's are, of course, the "*organization men.*" In orientation, little different from organization men in any institution, from the loyal "I wouldn't be anything but a Methodist" and "keep the show on the road" type, to the busy executives in the branch or front office. Loyal, dedicated churchmen, often giving their all to the maintenance of the church.

One characteristic of the institution-centered, that is, church-centered orientation, is its narrow definition of "ministry" as a career, something against which the more cause-oriented clergy continuously rebel. To protect itself from dilution, its representatives draw up official definitions and categories, in terms of tight roles in the institution. As Gene Reeves (Chapter VII above) discovered: "High denominational officials claim that if a man is going to be effective in the ministry, it has to be the only thing he really wants to do."

A–2's are the *reformers within:* "Her Majesty's loyal opposition." They have not given up on the church, but yearn for some change. In all denominations, at all levels of operation, in pulpits and administrative offices, they are hard at work, trying new approaches and pushing for new patterns.

B–1's are those who identify with the church so strongly, that when they're out, they're very much out. Feeling rejected, or at least cut off, they may, in reaction, make some gesture of denial themselves: repudiating their former profession by taking up a totally different kind of work, rejecting the church, or turning their backs on both.

B–2's are those out of the church but, in their own minds, "ministers still," discussed above in Chapter VII; cause-centered, following the star of the cause wherever it may lead them. They "hang loose" to the institution.

Many in this B–2 camp have training and certification in other fields, and are immediately employable as something other than minister: counselor, administrator, teacher, civil rights worker, and so forth. This reinforces the position and attitude of the cause-centered minister: caring less that he works in a church, than that he works effectively. His distinctiveness lies not in the specialty itself, but in his eagerness to use it in any context which will free him, and provide the opportunity for effective ministry. Not only is such a clergyman more able to leave the parish but, as studies of departing priests verify, because of his viewpoint, he is more willing. Understandably, many "ex-clergy" are not disturbed in the least that they work outside the blessed portals. This explains, too, the ease with which some clergy translate from parish and pulpit careers to secular ones.

Such a professional is Hobart Burch, a clergyman, graduate of Union Theological Seminary in New York City, with a master's degree and a Ph.D. in social welfare planning. When his denomination has an opening for his particular package of skills, he is delighted. He is delighted now, as Secretary of Health and Welfare for the United Church of Christ.

When it has no opening: no problem—he finds a job as an "outside minister." He spent the previous five years in the government in the National Institute of Mental Health in Washington, D.C. He moves in and out of the church comfortably and freely as the opportunities present themselves, and wherever he is, he is a minister.

The Tent-Maker. Another "new" category of minister making a place for itself today is the "tent-maker," spiritual descendant of St. Paul himself, and in this generation, the child of the French Catholic worker–priests of the 1940's. The tent-maker stands apart from our typology, or straddles it (perhaps an A/B?). Essential to his position and influence is that he maintains his commitment, as an ordained clergyman, to institutional religion (an A), while getting his bread (as a B) from a secular occupation.

The advantage of the tent-maker, as many are discovering, is that he has thus cut the economic root of psychological dependency. He may be uncritical of the religious establishment: content, for example, to celebrate the Eucharist on weekends for a congregation too small to support a full-time pastor. This makes him a promising ally to officialdom, worried by the bleak prospects for thousands of such parishes.

More important, however, is the tent-maker as an instrument of reform, both within the religious institution and in society. In himself he embodies prophetic religion divested of all that stultifies it in a "worldly" church: its stake in the economic and political status quo, its preoccupation with its own maintenance as an institution, its stereotypes of "ministry" which no longer meet people's deep needs.

Ivan Illich, the renowned Catholic reformer–seminarian, exemplifies the tent-maker approach and, indeed, advocates it as a strategy. He is sharply critical of the Church, at the same time citing chapter and verse of its own forgotten prophetic tradition against its present-day bureaucratic sins. Protestant reformers would agree: to them this approach is not only a personal solution to career problems but an instrument of renewal.

Vital Variable: Ministerial "Style"

If part of the clergyman's self-image is the degree to which he identifies with the church, another part is how he interprets his role. There are many possible versions, and many of them are sanctified: as a shepherd with sheep; as an understanding helper, adviser, counselor; as a spokesman for the Almighty; as a celebrant-priest; as an eminent authority; as a servant; a man for others; a pulpit pundit; and so on.

Much has been made of the conflict of roles—teacher *vs.* administrator *vs.* preacher *vs.* prophet—and of the impossibility of fulfilling all demands and expectations. Every clergyman, however, has an overall image of his own personal style. Though there is a great range of styles chosen, there is considerable evidence that personal styles, as a category, are undergoing change.

Such changes are in the direction of greater informality, less authoritarianism, more humanness, more "coach rather than quarterback," more enabler than star performer.

A 1966 study compared the personal statements of men coming into the ministry in the years 1961–1965 with those of persons entering the same ministry twenty years previously. The trend was unmistakably away from the "Great Dr. So-and-So" toward the image of catalyst and enabler. Typical of the newer statements were the following:

> The real job of the leader is to help the group define its own goals, and to help them to organize to solve their own problems in a ministry of all members.

.   .   .   .   .

The pulpit is not the expounder of a transmitted tradition but the privileged reporter of one's own studies and meditations.

. . . . .

As counselor, one is not the symbol of the moral code so much as a compassionate friend able to call on training and perspective.

. . . . .

As executive secretary one doesn't carry out the will of the congregation himself, so much as mobilize the far greater resources and talents.

. . . . .

The minister as teacher is more concerned with creating significant questions than providing stable answers.

A Jewish seminary professor suggested that only with this kind of change in the pattern of the rabbinate is it likely to survive.

Great Expectations

Part of the impact of Samuel Blizzard's findings on clergy performance ("The Minister's Dilemma") was his documentation of the startling discrepancy between ministerial expectations and realizations. Once settled in a parish, clergy find themselves performing tasks they least enjoy, least expected, and for which they are ill-prepared: administration, organization, budgeting, fundraising. There is too little opportunity for anticipated and more enjoyable roles, such as preacher, pastor, counselor, or teacher.

Later research pointed up their dilemma even further: the main time and energy of clergy are devoted to activities least appreciated by their own parishioners: i.e., administration. But while laity don't want their minister to be mickey-mouse, they provide very little wherewithal to relieve or prevent it.

What are the expectations of clergy as they enter upon their career? How do they define, and anticipate, the institution they will serve? The following are three statements of young clerics who began their pastorates in 1965, a decade after Blizzard, explaining their concept of the church in today's society:

> What is the church? The church is 1) a community of free people, and 2) a questioner and demander in society as against a rubber stamp for the status quo. It is the self-conscious bearer of a whole set of religious and social values, which it must try to actualize, in itself and in society.
>
> . . . . .
>
> The church is a community which has made explicit its central goal: the radically honest search for meaning and integrity in the face of all we face, as creatures of both glory and squalor.
>
> . . . . .
>
> The church is a focus of concern in community, a place where the conscience of the future is followed today. A breeder of institutions for causes. A catalyst. A multiplier of the vital energies of its members. Yet also a redemptive community able to provide the support every person needs in the process of growth from stultifying but comfortable conformity to creative but frightening freedom.

"Redemptive community" was the central idea in most statements from which this sample was taken.

The pressing question is, of course, will this new

generation of ministers find churches who share their vision, their companioning approach?

The answer depends upon how thoughtful and perceptive the congregation is, and how authoritarian its mode of operation. There are still so few churches of the genre described hopefully above, as to discourage seminarians, but more and more laymen are taking the nonauthoritarian approach. So much so, that many of them leave the church in disappointment, or in quest of more meaningful contexts. Most of these are then lost to institutional religion. A very few go on to form lay groups and "house churches."

Faint Realizations

The discrepancy between expectations and realizations may be greater for the ministry than for any other profession. Whether the expectations are unreasonable—too high—or the reality is unpredictably low, depends, no doubt, on the individual pastor and congregation. Is he a dreamer? Are they too wide of the mark? Whatever the explanation or cause, this discrepancy, rather than the many variables so painstakingly factored out, may be "the missing 'x' in Exodus."

Thus, the failure of the real-life situations in the parish to come up to expectations, indeed the contradiction of them, may be the crucial element in today's restlessness and defection.

There are other, more worldly disappointments as well.

Job Opportunities. Episcopalians have so many more clergy than viable openings that the suggestion has been offered that they quit turning out ministers until demand and supply are in balance. Unitarian Universalists have three persons seeking a new pulpit for every one vacant. As for

Catholics, "Many young priests are simply crushed by years of unproductive waiting. Ordained in their twenties, they often have to wait decades for the kind of responsibility that can come to laymen in a matter of years."

Salary Level. Clergy may not leave their parish posts for money reasons alone, but they will not stay for pay alone, either! American Baptists reported that the average salary for ministers in their retirement plan "was $7,666 as of February, 1969. This figure includes an allowance for housing . . . a family of four now needs an income of $9,900 to maintain a moderate living standard in an urban area." This is probably fairly good, as salaries for clergy go. The National Council of Churches reported some years earlier "the median clergy salary is less than the median salary for teachers, factory foremen, sales personnel, and salaried managers and officials."

It is no wonder that when clergy leave, their new secular jobs pay more: there is hardly any way to go but up.

Ladder with No Rungs. Even more basic and problematical than raises and openings is the small size of the typical congregation and the absence of a ladder. James Lowery, in a 1970 study of Episcopal parishes, found that sixty-two percent of them were too small to have any prospect except to be "programmed for exhaustion in survival." These congregations contained only one-seventh of the total membership, but required forty-five percent of the ministers. The situation is not likely to improve. Lowery points out that, for the churches he studied, it had been the same for the past fifteen years, the *peak* years of organized religion's prosperity, now declining.

The same situation obtains for many "main line" churches. Although much has been said and written about a "minister shortage," this occurs mostly among marginal congregations. In truth, there are not enough *viable* churches, that is, congregations offering a decent living, let alone opportunities for advancement, to clergy. For most pastors, no matter what their talents, if they go "where the Lord calls" (to what the bishop has available) there can be no moving up a ladder: there *is* no ladder. A graph of congregations by size and resources would be all bottom and no top. The institutional predestination of the man entering the ministry is a foreordained damnation more certain than theological predestination ever was.

Nevertheless, for all the complaints that the church has lost its vitality and mission in the world of today, for all the discrepancies and inadequacies just noted, young people continue to move into its ministry with the conviction that it still holds more promise than anything else.

And whatever their beefs, active clergy seem to feel the same. Asked to express their opinion on this statement: "The mission of the church can no longer be carried on effectively through the local congregation or parish church," a majority of parish and nonparish ministers in five denominations disagreed. In summarizing their attitudes (in his research report, *Changing Expectations and Ethics in the Professional Ministry*), Murray H. Leiffer concluded:

> Evidently pastors, even if they are discouraged about the local church, are convinced that there is more hope for the mandate of the Gospel to be manifested through such congregations and parish churches than by any other means.

The "Call" Outside

When clergy leave the parish, where do they go? Anywhere and everywhere, from poverty programs to real estate, from selling sports cars to the sensitivity training circuit.

The executive marketing firm, Earl Blue Associates, in 1970 reported that in almost every instance the occupational preferences of its ex-clergy clients continue to be centered on "serving the needs of other people," their choices clustering in one of three categories: counseling, education, and management.

As to where they actually wind up, however, no overall figures are available. Since there is no way of knowing accurately how many have left, no census is possible. Moreover, unlike his former self, the ex-clergyman is a low-visibility person: he evaporates. But some scattered estimates are available. Mrs. Roy, the Director, says that about fifty-five percent of the clients of Bearings in New York City go into people-helping occupations. The *Gallagher Presidents' Report* for January, 1969, citing a business-oriented survey of ex-priests, notes that half had gone into business, 27.3% into education, 13.6% into social service, and 6.8% into government.

In their *Ex-Pastors* investigation, Jud, *et al.*, listed in decreasing order of frequency, careers in social service and social change, education, professions, science and art, followed by business. About half of their total sample had gone into the education and service categories.

An American Baptist breakdown of 160 who left the parish in 1968 gives a similar, if imprecise, picture: sixty-seven into "industry, government or social service," forty-three into teaching, and the rest, scattered. The Unitarian Universalist Report on Ministerial Shifts for the years 1964 through 1968 shows almost half transferred to teaching or further study, and ten to fifteen percent each, to social welfare, nonchurch professional work, business, and the arts.

Overall impression: most "ex-pastors" are people-helpers still.

Back at the Parson Factory

One point, possibly the only point, on which everyone connected with the church seems agreed, is that there is something terribly wrong at the seminary. It is obviously not preparing ministers for the job they want to do, or have to do. Until it does, we will have square pegs in round holes.

New models are available for the seminary however. One at least has been on display for quite a while.

Something over twenty years ago, Josiah Bartlett became head of Starr King School for the Ministry in Berkeley, California. He had been drafted by the trustees on the basis of a report in which he declared that ministers were neither carefully chosen, nor well prepared, for their basic task of working with people. Their studies were cloistered. They needed to assimilate the findings of behavioral science, to move out of their isolation, to university classrooms and to life as it was lived. He immediately upgraded admissions standards so that seminarians could qualify for the neighboring University of California's graduate courses. He initiated screening for personality. Students were placed in community agencies and churches under close supervision. Classes shifted from note-taking to discussions; study plans were tailor-made according to the individual's readiness and previous experience.

Students were brought into decision-making at all levels, from admissions to passing on faculty and prospective graduates. They served on all administrative boards and committees. Seminarians who could convince their fellows they had enough to give (many came with advanced degrees and years of business experience) could offer courses of their own.

The building was enlarged and rebuilt as an art gallery. The new chapel had no fixed seats or furnishings, thus challenging students (who conducted the services) to experiment. A refresher program was added, to bring from the field ministers who could exchange experiences with students, and review their own situation and needs. Neighboring seminaries looked on the program as bizarre, and some shrugged it off as a "trade school." Even seminaries with which it was connected historically, such as Harvard, found it hard to take seriously. However, the experiment prospered.

At the start of a new decade, the 1970's, Harvey Cox of Harvard Divinity School predicted for the "seminary of the future" many of these same elements, and indeed, many seminaries have begun to move in this direction already, and on a massive scale.

Though many seminaries drag themselves with reluctance into the twentieth century, others, of all faiths, are in rapid transition: Jesuits at Woodstock and Franciscans at Santa Barbara pull up stakes and move to the city, and the ultimate of ultimates, the "Greg," Rome's pontifical Gregorian University, has broken out of its mold, dropped Latin for instruction, gone coed, put students on its curriculum committee, and, in the interest of ecumenism, added Protestants—a Southern Baptist theologian from Louisville, no less—to its faculty.

The day of the sequestered, denominationally provincial seminary is past: many have closed and more are closing. On the rise is the ecumenical seminary-cluster, such as the Boston Theological Institute, or Berkeley's Graduate Theological Union. The first has seven, the second ten, member schools of many faiths. They pool faculty, library, and study facilities, open courses freely to one another. As Cox describes it, "The coming generation of Catholic priests will have heard about Luther and Niebuhr directly from Protestant teachers and classmates, and Protestants will have studied St. Thomas and the social encyclicals with Catholic professors."

Furthermore, the lines between sacred and secular

subjects will become less important. The seminary cluster in Chicago has taken the city for its laboratory. Theology programs will blend into studies in secular universities; already students in some departments get credit for work in either institution.

The students knew something had to be done: as Bridston and Culver found, only thirty-three percent of entering seminarians, in 1965, expected to take the traditional path to the parish ministry. In the years since then, it is the students themselves who have forced open the old gothic windows to new ideas and atmosphere.

Retake on the Calling

"From beginning to end," sighed a discouraged churchman at a conference on the ministry, "there are so many holes and gaps to plug. Fixing up the ministry is like trying to patch a sieve!"

Repairs may be called for all along the line, but something is happening to the troubled old sieve. The most important development in the profession in this century is now taking shape: the emergence of a wholly new concept of ministry. The new concept breaks sharply from the old three-step model unquestioned for decades:

- the "call" to ministry, once received
- theological education
  (for some—by no means for all, even yet)
- a lifetime of work at the "calling"
  (until one drops or retires, whichever comes first)

This is the model that is now blowing up. It no longer works.

The new philosophy sees ministry as an infinitely complex and changing career. Not apart from the world, but of it. Therefore, open and in touch with the world's new knowledge, new developments. It must be continuously nourished, refueled, updated. There must be careful selection of those who enter it: many are called, but few should be chosen.

The new philosophy sees "preparation" as ongoing and continuous; a long-term proposition, no longer a preliminary dosage or a one-shot seminary rite. It sees not only the need for refreshment but for personal reassessment as one goes. It sees the clergy as a useful, capable, and creative slice of humanity, with its own needs and problems, not the least of which are immediate and personal needs, of themselves and their families, to be ministered unto.

This revolutionary philosophy is not revolutionary at all for other professions or for the business world, where the necessity for retooling and refreshment has been taken for granted for years.

In the ministry, "continuing education" is not only a late-comer, trailing far behind, but has simply meant more of the same seminary fare: courses, reading programs, and lectures for credit. Now, as the new philosophy emerges, it is coming to mean individualized programs of personal and professional advancement—not simply academic—focused on the pastor as a productive human being, for whom career can be a vehicle of fulfillment as a person. A new literature is emerging in which are spelled out the philosophic underpinnings, tentative blueprints, and plans for such an educational program.

The most ambitious of these projects so far is a three-year study by the United Presbyterians, culminating in a formidable 1969 "Blue Book." In presenting its recommendations, its study commission designated continuing education as "*basic to the work of the whole church and not simply (a) peripheral program for the benefit of interested clergymen.*"

A top level Episcopal group has also developed (1969) a position paper, which declares that "Continuing education should provide a stage for the open recognition of professional personal problems and the avoiding of the anguish of private and hopeless struggles with them."

Almost overnight there has been an explosion of papers and consultations and reports, programs and experiments, in continuing education for the clergy, which includes formation of "SACEM"—the Society for the Advancement of Continuing Education for the Clergy.

If continuing education is now big, big also is career counseling for ministers. The pioneer Northeast Career Center got under way at Princeton, New Jersey, in 1967. To it now are being added others: the Midwest Career Development Center in Columbus, Ohio, is patterned on much the same model. With career counseling, the Baptists have combined, at their Wellesley Hills Center, continuing education, guidance, and placement service, as well as salary support. In July, 1970, with support from other denominations, they opened a Western Church Career Center in Oakland, California. Still others are on the drawing boards.

Within individual denominations, these ideas are taking hold. "In this denomination," says Albert Haversat of the Lutheran Church of America, "the career development emphasis is being 'bought.' It's a major shift from 'mere education' to 'career development.' By the end of 1970, $150,000 to $200,000 will probably have been spent by Lutherans alone on various aspects of clergy career development."

The Career Development Council, new ecumenical coordinating body of which Haversat is treasurer, was initiated by the forward-looking Department of Ministry in the National Council of Churches. It "conservatively" estimates an expenditure of over two and a half million dollars by 1975 for clergy career development.

The overall aim, Haversat concludes, is "a total system of career help and guidance through seminary, to be picked up at any point in later life. In short, what we are trying to build is a continuing human process."

Other holes in the sieve are also being filled. To relieve "the anguish of private struggles," a network of resources is being developed for individual and specialized needs, psychiatric, marital, family, and other. One center deals with clerical alcoholism alone. A pioneer resource is Interpreter's House at Lake Junaluska, North Carolina, with its guru Carlyle Marney. With Methodist funding and Baptist aid for scholarships, it gives help in rubbing off the edges of clerical uptightness, or working through crises: faith, drinking, homosexuality.

Group process resources are springing up as well: specialized programs and techniques for ministers in all sectors of church relations and operation: conflict management, human relations training, human potential development. A typical example is seminars in church executive development for "senior ministers in multi-staffed local congregations." Much of the knowhow comes from secular specialists, those prepared by the National Training Laboratories, established by the National Education Association.

Self-improvement programs, under the new (1968) Academy of Parish Clergy in Minneapolis, are developing stature. No longer is the ministry "the only profession without its own association to develop its own standards of vocational competence."

It is a contention of many who counsel clergy today that a considerable portion of those who dropped out did not need to leave—should not have left, perhaps. They simply did not have the help when they needed it: some reassurance and strengthening of their convictions, some updating of their insights and techniques, or just some understanding someone to talk with at a critical moment. Should anyone doubt the significance of this overdue shot in the arm for the long-suffering clergy, here is a note penned by one of them on returning from a refresher–reassessment interlude with fellow clergy:

> This was the most important two weeks of my ministry. I got a new lease on my career, a healthy dose of perspective and balance. I'll be living on this capital for many years to come.

CHAPTER NINE

New Bells and New Bottles

Things look bleak for the church. The 1970's dawned with a dark mood indeed: "The church is sick." "Religion is dying." To top it off, the clergy exodus. But look again. Much of the "bad" is good. Much of the tearing down, necessary. Dead wood, yes—but new green shoots are showing everywhere.

Look again at the Exodus. The exodus is growing: from all sectors of the church, all parts of the country. It is threatening, accelerating. Where are all the parsons vanishing? Some, to be sure, *are* simply vanishing: into offices and bureaus and agencies, into a thousand little corners of business and industry. More still are going into teaching and welfare and social work.

Look at Herschel and Paul and George and James—their real names. Each of them went from a "standard" ministry in a "standard" congregation to a ministry that is "real" for him. "I'm a dropout rabbi," says Herschel Lymon, with an engaging smile. He dropped out from the organization-man temple "thing." Happy, excited, his life revolves around sharing an exuberant wisdom of living as a staff member in a new kind of counseling clinic. Lymon has found himself: he went through both the "temple builder" and the flaming social prophet stages. He looks like a movie idea of a prophet now: lean, strong, hair flying in all directions, dark burning eyes. But there is something different: a lightness, buoyancy. "I used to be a heavy," he says, "I *was* heavy. Had that rabbi look—serious, worried, uptight, frightened. Not now. It's all in learning how to let go. I learned to be *empty:* do you know what I mean?"

"Subconsciously," he went on. "I wanted out. So I got myself fired: 19 to 0. Unanimous! I'm not bitter; I should have been fired. The institution is *finis*. I couldn't possibly return to it. Occasionally I do some ceremonies for friends, when they grow out of live situations." He described a funeral: a prayer, an informal talk about what the body means, and spirit. "We held hands around, and we hallowed that plot of ground. 'When you get home,' I said, 'you'll feel it's all all right.' And it was so."

Lymon hasn't lost his social conscience, but explains "I no longer think in the old liberal *vs.* radical terms. Now it's old *vs.* new: aware or unaware." One is not astonished to find he got his awareness the hard way. Eighteen years of analysis "got just nowhere." He has visited all the meccas of personal growth and awareness—Esalen, Kairos—and learned from them. "Awareness" and "human potential" are part of his vocabulary: awakening people to their potential, "young people especially; people changing careers."

"Really the man who turned me on was Weininger." Dr. Benjamin Weininger heads the Southern California Counseling Clinic, Herschel Lymon's base. Just as his is a new kind of rabbinate, so this is a new kind of clinic. "We took seriously the suggestion of some National Institute of Mental Health research: that intuitive housewives could do as good a job, maybe better, helping people with their problems, than the experts."

Under Dr. Weininger's orientation and supervision, some eighty instructed lay counselors serve the clinic. Clients pay ten dollars an hour if they can afford it; those who are broke pay nothing. Naturally there was scandalized opposition at first; little now. The clinic fits exactly a spot left blank elsewhere: help for ordinary troubles, of ordinary people who can't afford what professionals must charge. Lymon is one of several more thoroughly trained staff people who bind the operation together and take on chores they can best perform.

Herschel Lymon is a new kind of rabbi. "There has to be something better than the institution," he feels. And for himself, he seems to have found it.

*Allons! after the great Companions, and to
belong to them! They too are on the road . . .*

Whitman's lines are no metaphor to Paul Sawyer. Afoot and lighthearted, his *is* the open road. A wandering ministerial minstrel, he is apt to show up anywhere: working and resting a while on Ken Kesey's farm, traveling with a commune to the Woodstock music festival. Handsome, long hair gathered like Leatherstocking's, having found the parish is not his bag, Paul is poet, artist, writer, speaker, moviemaker, and singer of the new–old religion of the contemporary scene.

No doubt striking most people as one who rejects his culture, Sawyer is in fact self-consciously steeped in it. He was the precocious, self-reliant student who worked his way through Harvard in three years. His "great companions" are Whitman, Emerson, William Carlos Williams, e. e. cummings, and Charles Olson—and their kindred spirit Dante. "To sing America must be an ACT of LOVE," wrote Paul,

For what it was
For what it is
For what it is to be.

"Since I began my ministry here to this congregation at twenty-four, never having been a minister before, there was a lot to be learned," he wrote.

> I could keep on asking myself, 'What does a
> minister do?' For a long time it didn't occur to me
> to ask, 'What do I Paul Sawyer do?' 'Who am I
> above, beyond and including my work as a
> minister?' . . . And the answers are not to be
> given from the outside—(for instance, by finding
> out what a minister is)—but only from the inside
> by finding out what kind of a person we are, what
> we enjoy doing, what gives meaning to us
> personally. . . . I too 'Midway in our life's
> journey went astray from the straight road and
> woke to find myself alone in a dark wood.'

Paul's quest, for a time, was an Inferno for himself, his family, his people. He would not want to say he has climbed his mountain yet, only

> *I am Paul*
> *a little older, not running*
> *quite so fast,*
> *happier and sadder*
> *Not as sure, but more sure of Paul.*

He has tried to write of Los Angeles and Seattle as William Carlos Williams wrote of Paterson and Charles Olson wrote of Gloucester. His ministry—he considers it fully, self-consciously that—one could say is the interpreter of America to itself, poet of the people's faith: teacher, preacher who drops in to congregations, or makes his own.

George Johnson is a big man, a powerful man with a great voice, booming out the memory of his poem *Harlem of My Childhood* to help "make church people religious." Johnson knows how to live in two worlds, black and white. He has served three white Methodist congregations, in fact: "Now *there* was discrimination in *reverse:* whatever I wanted I got, just because I wanted it."

As a church-supported civil rights worker, George moved westward, through the most troubled cities in their most troubled times: Cleveland, Chicago, Los Angeles. He knows the intellectual, rationalist coldness of most whites. Nevertheless, he accepted from ministers of white suburban congregations a plea to organize the East Bay Project in Oakland's black ghetto. This project combats white racism in the suburbs, and channels suburban congregations' support for black empowerment in the city. No one knows better than he the risks this involves, when, as now to militant blacks, any taint of whiteness means sellout. His Project's board is deliberately black-dominated, with white approval. His work shifts and twists with the turns and deepening crisis of black despair and white unresponsiveness. George walks a thin, uncertain line. It is a lonesome road, but one he has to walk.

James Reeb began life about as far from the historic civil rights confrontation in Selma, Alabama, as one can imagine: in the big sky country of central Wyoming. He moved through two denominations: Presbyterian and Unitarian, and out of the parish to take a post in a ghetto in Boston. His meager salary was supplied by a denomination which has no ministers: the Friends, in a Service Committee experiment.

Reeb was one of the hundreds who answered the call of Martin Luther King in the early 1960's, when there was bright hope that white oppression might yield to the pleas of conscience. Jim never saw that hope denied; brightness for him, all brightness, was put out by the bludgeon of a defender of the dark, who struck him down on a rainy street in Selma and left him dying.

Dropouts? Anti-religion? Who could be more "minister" than these?

The Cracked Crock

Several years ago a seminary professor built a book on the assertion—apparently news even to this age—that the church like other institutions, is human. "For all its treasure," he exclaimed, "the church is an earthen vessel! God has chosen to immerse it in the life of the world. Because it is in the world, it shares the conditions and experiences of all communities."

Too few, apparently, see that the church is an earthen, inescapably human vessel. In many voices, those quitting the church agree: "The crock is cracked!" They whisper and shout, they mope and rage, they withdraw and defy, they explain and denounce, but on this they agree. They see the old structures as outworn, the old models as useless. They raise their voices against the unyielding tradition, the strangling stereotypes, the ears that hear not, the hearts that do not feel.

They cry out against solemn prayers in the church while Rome and its people burn. They cry out against the barriers it creates between itself and reality. They cry out against its imperviousness to persons, themselves and their concerns included. They, and some of those still hanging on, declare that churches and their old devices are not only useless, but obstacles that stand in the way of the living religion, the new creed.

In their book on the failure of church renewal, Lecky and Wright mince no words:

- "The church does not trust God or man."

- "It is precious in its own sight."

- "The decent thing for church institutions would be to die."

- "Religion is too important to be left any longer to the churches."

Men at Work

Happily, those who leave are not content with lamentation. More than one would believe, they are hard at work fashioning new vessels, different from the old ones, and from one another's. One of their first tasks must be to tear down the Great Wall, that improbable barrier between the "sacred" and the "secular." "There *is* no 'sacred' or 'secular,'" the workers cry. "The sacred is everywhere! And outside the church is 'in.' The new wine must flow freely through the world, where it will."

"Chairman Jesus" in Charge. Among those chipping away at this wall is a small band of workers in the Land of the Young Lords of East Harlem. Taking their orders from "Chairman Jesus," ten people, three of them former priests, are out to destroy the old barricade between world and church, and put something else in its place. They call it Emmaus House.

There are dozens of such communities and communes—living groups, parareligious experiments, clans of "Jesus freaks." But this particular community has a gift for sorting out false starts and misconceptions, for inventing effective ways of working together, so as to help all who are similarly engaged.

Self-conscious, imaginative, and articulate, they can

serve to capsule the experience, and to some extent, to speak
for them all.

"What began as a simple house of hospitality meta-
morphosed into a communal experience. A journey into the
unknown, involving the risk of pilgrimage without resting
station." Thus, says one of its resident members: "Emmaus
House became our setting for entering into this experience
of change. We institutionalized change."

Both the church and the world are, as the members
of this "venture in community and communication" see it,
in an Emmaus situation, that is, in an event in process. Church
is not in a building, but in lives. "Our experience is an end in
itself." In this way do the residents of Emmaus House see
themselves as a constantly changing, constantly growing
community. Emmaus is many things, they explain: being, doing, belonging, relating, communicating, growing, changing,
creating, laughing, crying, playing, listening, sharing, serving,
celebrating, liberating.

Observers and reporters try to capsule and categorize
the center in black and Puerto Rican East Harlem, on 116th
Street, in terms that everyone knows: "underground church,"
a revolutionary community, a commune. But the members of
Emmaus House resist categorizing. "No stereotypes" they
say, "not even the newest."

We cannot see ourselves associated with the
so-called 'underground church' movement as it is
presented today. Nor can we rush from one fad to
another just to be 'in' and 'with it.' Catholic
renewal is simply too nervous. We see ourselves as
a radical community which is not out to shoot
down bishops, but rather to be a setting for human
life and service. We are not ready to canonize any
answers coming out of today's church, nor do we

want to become separate and elitist. We want to
be free for responsible experimenting, open to the
past which has a vote, and the possibilities of
breaking through to completely new territory in
the future.

"Being," that is, meditation, celebration, and play,
takes an equal place with "doing," that is, service and action.
And "doing your own thing" is inevitably doing for others.
Thus, Emmaus House is a "house of hospitality" where
3,500 people a year come by, to share words, bread, or bed,
as needed. Many come because they need a place to live.
Many come because they need a place to stay until they get
a job. A few are lonely and simply need to talk. Others wish
to share common concerns. The services range from a school
for East Harlem children, to a problem clinic, a draft counseling project, and a center for urban encounter. Emmaus
House is a fellowship, a brotherhood, not an experimental
parish. It has no experimental liturgy: its liturgy is spontaneous. It is not out to reform the church; it is an alternative to
the church. The experiment started in 1966. They wrote on
the wall a saying of Bonhoeffer: "We will not know what
we will not do."

In one sense, Emmaus House is not a house. It is a
spiritual center of concentric circles. In the middle is the
East Harlem commune: ten persons who have a daily intensive and sharing experience.

In what they call "temporary patterns for a temporary community" they agree

. . . to search for an authentic human life, to
make community the place for personal and social
transformation, for actuating human potential, for
creativity. We agree to search for a 'torah,' a way

of life with others . . . for a secular affirmation
of Christian and humanist values. We agree to
search for a radical style, to take sides, affirming
life against death, humanness against oppression.
. . . We agree to search for the living God, in
the focus of new relationships in Christ, through
human experiences now and in history.

There is a continuous process of self-evaluation and self-criticism.

A somewhat larger circle, of perhaps thirty individuals scattered over the city, come together periodically for the "agape"—common meals, common work, and a common search for "a truly human life-style for Manhattan 1970."

Outside this circle is still another: task force groups of seventy-five or so persons; these come together each week in work communities around an issue or special project. One such project was a celebration, much misunderstood at the time: an "anti-Christmas festival" in December, 1969. The intent was to celebrate the real meaning of Christmas and, at the same time, to protest against its commercialization. Part of the festival was a march around St. Patrick's Cathedral with horns and banners.

Finally, the largest concentric circle consists of supporters and friends of the House, who share their own vision as well as their skills, knowledge, and money. They are kept in touch, in part, through the Emmaus publication, *The Bread Is Rising*, which was a word of whispered hope among peasants of the French Revolution.

Emmaus was founded by David Kirk, now coordinator, a priest of the Melkite Byzantine rite. There is, however, no cult of personality of the founder. Two other priests are a part of the commune: Richard Mann and Tom Phillips, but no titles are ever used, and seniority is never discussed among them. Their views on ministry:

While some of us would not use theological terms
like 'ministry,' it is useful to describe the situation.
We are trying to develop a single ministry, a
composite of different people serving in different
functions (ministries): myself, as coordinator and
enabler for tasks and people, i.e., David Kirk;
Richard Mann as celebrator and editor; Kathy
Mahon as educator; Bob Lowe as community
organizer, and so on. Together we share a common
ministry of availability, listening, being present,
being available, and exploration.

Authority then is based on function: communal and co-
ordinated.

We have many questions, not many answers. Like
the disciples on the road to Emmaus, we are
searching. We risk the unknown, putting
everything to the test. [Ours] are the notes of
fellow-searchers, with the rest of men, sharing
what we have experienced and discovered so far.
'Like one beggar who tells another beggar where
to find bread.'

JOURNEY

Funny things happened to us on the way to Emmaus.
We became fellow-travellers with all kinds of
people, recognizing
Jesus, incognito, in friendship, in the breaking of
bread, the sharing of words and reality.
People came and left, and others came.
We made community, worked, had fun.
Seeds became oaks, children became men.
New ways of life broke through.
Myths were shattered and realities were dimly seen.
Pet ideologies burst open.

> *Options opened up: creating reasons for existence,*
> *or writing a poem or starting a school or joining*
> *a political party.*
> *Funny things happened on the way to Emmaus*
> *and, thank God, it is still happening.*

The Holy Grail. For an astonishing number of seekers, the Holy Grail that they search for is a "viable alternative to the church." The "alternative" may be a commune, an extended family or utopia, an underground church, a house church, or a new type church-non-church built from scratch.

A California clergyman, Richard Fairfield, has staked out a personal and unique ministry: seeking out these utopias. Organizer of the Alternatives! Foundation, he issues an *Alternatives Newsletter*, a pictorial newspaper of the "underground/alternative press," a paper called *Vision*, and *The Modern Utopian*, a quarterly magazine about communes. Fairfield also puts out directories of and for communes, free schools, and experimental colleges, organizations for social change, personal growth, nudism, and sex. Though he is the first to admit that he cannot keep up and his listings are incomplete, the sheer number of items in his directories is startling evidence of the "rising bread."

Repairs and Remodeling, Inc. Some of those who, by choice or otherwise, have no present place within the church, have chosen as their task to repair the church from the *outside*. Such a one is the excommunicate priest, Thomas Durkin, who, as executive secretary of the Society of Priests for a Free Ministry, devotes himself full time to a movement for reform and purification.

Durkin grew up in the docile, repressed diocese of Philadelphia, where the whole thrust is toward unthinking obedience. He rebelled, and is proud to claim that he encouraged a seminary revolt which coined the phrase "underground church." He and other daring souls celebrated the English Mass in an underground enclave of the vast St. Charles Borromeo, before the official language was shifted from Latin.

For his sins, Durkin was "cooled" by being sent to a retreat for, among others, priests who have problems with drink or women or other scandalous conduct. But he was not cooled a bit: he married Gail, a Lutheran girl, and got a job in urban redevelopment. He turned down the idea of petitioning for "laicization" because "it's like cooperating with your draft board if you don't believe in the whole process"; turned down, too, a better job in favor of working for the "movement." He and Gail (and their infant son) hope to found a community: "You can't be fully a person by yourself."

In other days, Durkin would have left, if not secretly, at least in shame. Not so today. Standing with him are more than a thousand in the United States alone, technically both "out" and "in" who through the Society of Priests for a Free Ministry would ". . . contribute in a concrete and experimental way to a far-reaching renewal movement of the Church's ministry." Durkin has by no means left. His Society boldly ministers—among others, to the Church itself! It declares that it "looks forward to the official recognition of its ministry by the Roman Catholic Church. In the meantime, members of the Society will continue to serve the Church according to their unique gifts and . . . the various needs of local communities."

Another outside repairman is Robert Duggan, devoting himself to the reform of Roman Catholic rulings on celibacy. His vehicle is the National Association for Pastoral Renewal, of which he has been national coordinator. His view is that if the Church can face up to the celibacy issue and work it through, it can resolve anything.

Still another, completely different, church-repair outfit is the Episcopal team: Jones B. Shannon, John Soleau, and Henry Sherrill. They combine contemporary business knowhow with imaginative devotion to the church as an institution in desperate need of it. Jones Shannon grew bored with making money as a stockbroker, and at forty-six went into the ministry; later, a business consultant. Soleau has a business school background, taught pastoral theology, and, among other community experiences, helped manage Rockefeller's presidential primary campaign. Sherrill served as rector of several top echelon city parishes, with more than the usual community and denominational involvements that go with them.

They founded their firm, Consultation/Search, "so far as we know the only consultant outfit like it" to bring to churches and other voluntary organizations "the capacity to identify a problem and resolve it . . . the church is typically interested in problem *removing* not problem solving." Along with "hard nosed analysis" they bring an equal insistence on democratic responsibility. They would agree with Kenneth Boulding's lines applied to the church:

> *In every giant corporation*
> *Are channels of communication,*
> *Along which lines, from foot to crown,*
> *Ideas flow up and vetoes down.*

"The patriarchal model has had it," they conclude. "People want to make their own decisions."

Though the renewers and repairers have independent channels, very often their paths cross and their works merge.

Thus, the originator of the "underground church" is the executive of the Society of Priests for a Free Ministry, and this in turn is a spinoff of the celibacy reform organization, the National Association for Pastoral Renewal: a natural connection, since many of the priests are out in the cold because they acted to end their individual celibacy! The first conference of the SPFM was held in the Center for Christian Renewal in Washington, which had been established as a base for their fellow-priests, evicted for their stand on birth control. A board member of the SPFM is a founder of Crossroads, an association for renewal and reconciliation in Boston, with aims similar to those of New York's Emmaus House.

Their modes and philosophies differ. Some are loners, some, like the men in Consultation/Search, work in teams. And some, like Tom Durkin's team, are both in *and* out. They touch that ponderous old elephant, the church, each from his own side, and prod what they find to be its most sensitive point. This becomes their place and cause.

Were they concerned that the church is impersonal and uncaring? Then this becomes their call. Were they outraged by autocracy and lack of due process? Then they set about organizing a clergy union. Were they frustrated by meaningless forms and irrelevant ritual? If so, they may now walk with Malcolm Boyd or promote folk-rock masses. Are they pained by the church's performance gap? Perhaps they are then dedicating themselves to life in the ghetto, draft counseling, civil rights, race issues.

Not all who have left the church, then, have left. They are with it still, in one or another of its multiform definitions: as an individual or in a yet undefined ministry, in a brand new from-the-ground-up association, in a rebuild-the-church project.

No summary or sampling can do justice to the richness and variety of these "new ministries." One can only observe that through them, people now have the chance to use their very special talents: in the ghetto, in pressure groups, the suburb, the legislative hall; counseling, writing, speaking, organizing—whatever, wherever it is needed; that the new ministries cut through the traditional role conflicts. They cut through the stereotypes, cut out the nonessential. They drop fundraising. They drop pastoral calling (in the small group, people are already *there*). People are *themselves*, not acting like ministers.

Their tone is different: spontaneous, informal. Celebration almost always replaces traditional "worship"; flexibility, full range of media and "a *joyful* noise" are keynotes. The mood of these "liberated" clergy is different, too: their new enjoyment and satisfaction; their sense of escaping futility, of using their talents for something worthy; above all, their sense of being where they *should* be: "I'm doing what I really *feel!* I couldn't be happier!"

The Church Fights Back

The embattled old church has taken some body blows. It is reeling, but it hasn't given up. Some of its own, with ears to hear, have caught the message of the departing. Some inside its walls are taking to heart the dictum: heal thyself. On many fronts these loyal troops do battle. Some of the lost and departed cohorts are even drifting back to help.

Marching Song. Ideologically, the expression of loyal renewalism calls itself "the theology of hope." Its most "in" exponent—as is usually the case in the church's search for legitimation—is a German, Jürgen Moltmann. Moltmann takes his place now along with Harnack, Weber, Barth, Bonhoeffer, and Bultmann. His function is, as theirs was, to provide for church people a theological rationale for the church's adaptation to the changing scene and its needs. And as always, from its rich accumulation of scripture and theology, the church "reaches into its treasury and brings forth things new and old."

The new–old thing in this case is the rather obvious truth that, before it became assimilated to the secular society, the Church was a revolutionary force. As Moltmann expresses it,

> The task of Christianity today is not so much to oppose the ideological glorification of things, but rather to resist the institutional stabilizing of things, and by 'raising the question of meaning' to make things uncertain and keep them moving and elastic in the process of history.

So, church people find ideological leverage in all the judgmental elements of the original Biblical and early church tradition: the Last Judgment, the New Jerusalem, God as Lord of History, God's people as in Exodus from the corrupt Egypt of this world. The danger here is as obvious as the rationale—is all this mere rhetoric?

The earnest devotees of the "theology of hope" are working to make it more than just hope. No less than the remodelers outside, they are working on many fronts and in many ways to realize their dream of a church renewed.

Some Start with the Parson. "Putting first things first" means help for the parson—*before* his back is to the wall, before he drops out. This is the view of John Harris, Director of Continuing Education for the Episcopal Diocese of Washington, D.C. The help the clergyman needs, Harris declares, will be different at different stages of his career. Citing Donald Super's seminal work, *The Psychology of Careers*, he notes that the minister, like others, passes through career stages—a period of establishment, mid-career, maturity —in each of which his personal and professional needs differ; for each of which help should be available.

Furthermore, "We must recognize that the parish minister today is not a generalist and that the parish ministry today is one of highly specialized roles." Today the clergyman

> requires an ability to communicate in altogether new modes which can authentically connect with people's current living. Ministers must use a new kind of educational skill: one which assists people to explore and to interpret the meaning of their life-experience. Ministers must become competent in skills of sociological analysis, interdisciplinary planning, the use of consultants, collaboration in community program implementation.

> Today's pastor, far more than his predecessor, must know how to work collaboratively as a kind of broker, who utilizes professionals in other fields to meet the needs of the congregation and community.

Harris is one of those who adopts and takes seriously the "new philosophy of ministry." So, too, is his career, which is part of the growing network of clergy-help programs and resources—everywhere: continuing education, career consultation, counseling agencies.

Special resources and referral systems for clergy and their wives are emerging, almost month by month. It amounts to a long overdue, but hearteningly rapid, updating of the ministry as a career.

At this rate, it seems safe to predict that by 1975, there will be a reversal of the lonesome, frustrating, "no place to go" situation which now figures so importantly in clergy defection.

Some Parsons Start with Themselves. In 1965, the Rev. Granger E. Westberg, Dean of the Institute of Religion at the Texas Medical Center, wrote:

> Prodded into action by the growing number of medical specialists who made disparaging remarks to the effect that the general practitioner was not keeping up to date in medicine, a small group of G. P.s a few years ago organized the American Academy of General Practice. They even went a step beyond the specialists, requiring that all physicians who become members must engage each year in approximately 50 hours of postgraduate study approved by the academy.

"Could it be," Westberg asked, "that it is time to initiate a similar organization designed to encourage lifelong study by pastors?"

In 1968, the final holdout, the "only profession without its own association to develop standards of vocational competence," gave in. It established the Academy of Parish Clergy. Following the guidelines Westberg had suggested, the Academy was opened for business in July, 1969.

It has at last become possible for the 250,000 parish clergy in the United States to update their knowledge and skills within a bona fide professional context.

As clergy increasingly accept professional standards for their work, they are gradually becoming emboldened to ask for the conditions and equipment which will make professional-quality work possible. "A good workman deserves good tools."

Difficult though it may be to shake loose from the clerical stereotypes to which they have been conditioned— the "povre persoun," the "suffering servant," the unworldly martyr—clergymen are beginning to expect and ask for better pay, better hours, adequate office help—even contracts. To help one another in this uphill task—in which they are their own worst enemies—they are starting to strengthen one another in more militant clergy "unions."

Emerging, too, is a new type of parson who knows who he is and where he is going; who has the skills and contemporary consciousness Harris talks about. Here are three of them: one in Pennsylvania, one in Massachusetts, one in California:

Methodist Robert Raines of Germantown (Philadelphia) has consciously changed his stance and his style. He used to be a "prophetic loner," he explains, but sees himself now as an "enabling-type minister" who helps his congregation of more than 1,000 members carry out its own prophetic role. "When I came here," he says, "the church needed to be turned around. But the laymen are now sensitized. I don't have to be out on every picket line any more. The people are exercising *their* ministry."

Harold R. Fray, Jr., has met, head-on, the challenge of factional conflict in his congregation. He is minister of Eliot Church (United Church of Christ) in Newton, Massachusetts. Located in a pleasant white suburb of a major city, its building, history, membership composition, and ethos are all strikingly similar to a thousand other suburban churches. Harold Fray, however, is aware of who he is and what he is about. He is one of those who has not taken the popular stand.

"Must the minister of a local church win a popularity contest before he can be accepted as a leader?" he asks. He has not tried to please everyone, but has stood firmly on the liberal side of social involvement and action. His book, *Conflict and Change in the Church*, tells the story of his ministry, without glossing over the strong and continuous conflict, not only parishioners with pastor, but laymen with one another. The point of the story is that Fray did not, like so many, lose his job. Instead, by using conflict management skills, he was able to put the tensions to creative use.

Fray would agree with John Harris that today's minister needs training in such skills. But the seminary, until now anyway, has given him instead a prima donna self-image, feeding his temptation to arrogance. In order to create a sense of the whole ministry of the whole church,

> stress must be given to the minister as a *technician*. He must be taught skills commensurate with his responsibility as a leader and coach of the team in the local church. To be an enabler, to help others discover their ministry . . . there must be a sensitivity to *timing*. There is no need to force issues, or artificially to create situations for the sake of pushing some purpose or program along. Premature timing means picking the fruit too soon, when it is green and bitter. Procrastination means waiting until a situation rots.

> As for authority, according to congregational polity, authority on matters of policy and decision rests with the congregation. That does not resolve the issue of authority that centers around the minister. He has authority by being in a position to exert great influence.

Another minister who has done a total retake of himself and his way of working, in mid-career, is Karel Botermans.

Botermans is a thoughtful, deeply conscientious minister in a Unitarian Fellowship in "marvelous Marin"—on a green hilltop in the lush residential county just across the Golden Gate Bridge from San Francisco. His church's prob-

lem is precisely that it does have everything going for it—
location, affluent community, exciting people.

An able preacher, Karel found that for his people,
living as they do in the multimedia age, troubled as they are
by the meaninglessness of luxury, the conventional service-
with-sermon, the conventional round of activities wasn't
making it. He offered to resign; his people wouldn't hear of
it: "Take a year off," they said, "and explore new ways. If
you can't succeed as our minister, nobody can!"

On his return, Botermans explored his thinking with
his people. The result was a thoughtful transformation of
program, away from the old "come hear our preacher" approach, to a focus on people's needs, largest of which, perhaps, is genuine companionship. "Dialogue Between Parents
and Children" and "Deepening Awareness in Relationship
for Married and Unmarried Couples" are typical themes.
The congregation has instituted action projects in Marin
City (a festering slum the county would like to forget), en-
listed top talent for fun with an accent: Greek cookery
(shared in a festive spirit at the church or on somebody's
patio); yoga, and a Sunday "education program" whose
keynote is people sharing with people what turns them on.

Botermans' new ministry called for a new kind of
Sunday service, providing more participation for his people
than passive listening to his "performance." It begins, like a
Friends meeting, with some minutes of silence. Then the
minister encourages individuals to say what is most on their
mind—problem or joy or concern. He gets consensus on
which of these themes the people would like to take up.
There follows a thoughtful, deeply felt, person-to-person
sharing of ideas, wisdom, comfort, with the minister acting
as facilitator rather than "authority." The service flows
easily into a simple meal of bread and soup or coffee, little
knots of newly intimate people continuing their exchange.

This service carries out the notion of a shared ministry. It builds on what every pastor knows: that on any theme, there are a dozen who can speak to it better than he ever can in a monologue. (It should be added, that Botermans has not totally abandoned the conventional sermon. He preaches once a month still: "a far better sermon," he adds, "because it comes more directly from our common life, and because I have time to prepare it.")

Botermans' plan takes some practice and adjustment. Yet it is not so far from the familiar as to be unsettling for newcomers. It has the merit of allowing the worshiper to decide for himself how far he wishes to enter in. Finally, it presents the minister in his authentic role: as a real person, whose "authority" is precisely what his presence and mediatorial function convey.

From this service come, very often, the beginnings of personal ties, among the people with themselves and with the minister: much more than the conventional service with its hand shake at the door can yield.

Some Start with the Seminary. As many of those trying to rehabilitate the church have found, it is not enough to patch up the parson. They must push back even further: to the school which trained him. Few parts of the institutional structure are more under fire or in more transitional ferment today than the seminary.

As we have seen, the day of the isolated seminary "on a green hill far away" is over. In the perspective of history, attempting to remove the theological school far from the corrupting influence of the world, or the unsettling milieu of the secular university, appears as a colossal mistake.

So today Jesuit Alma College has moved from its once-rural Los Gatos, California, hilltop, and the Franciscan School of Theology from its historic site at Santa Barbara

Mission, to the ten-school ecumenical complex adjoining the University of California in Berkeley. Similar clusters have formed in Boston, St. Louis, Chicago, New York, and Washington.

Revolutionary changes are taking place in curriculum, also. The American Association of Theological Schools has presented a totally new model, incorporating case and clinical learning methods, extensive use of "real life" field situations, and the concept of teaching staff as resource persons and fellow-learners, rather than gowned authority figures lecturing from podiums.

The San Francisco Theological Seminary (Presbyterian) is a case in point. In 1963 it proudly initiated "a new curriculum designed to meet the needs of the Church in a new era." In 1969 it announced that "after scarcely three classes had been graduated under its contours, a *radically new design, more advanced, even revolutionary*, is being announced for inception in September of 1969." (italics supplied) "Traditional theological education," it observed, "prepared men and women for the *ministry*. This new design . . . prepares students for *ministries*."

This seminary is clearly responding not only to the changing church, but to the chief impetus for change within seminaries: the students themselves who, more and more, are frankly rejecting the parish and reaching for new ministries. The students have enough faculty and alumni on their side to effect change, though tradition, buttressed by endowments supporting overstuffed chairs in traditional stuffy subjects, yields but slowly.

At a symposium for all brands of Judaism on the future of seminary training for rabbis (May, 1969), chairman Arnold Jacob Wolf declared:

It is impossible any longer to pretend that our students are the compliant, careerist young

seminarians that they once were. . . . A few
years ago the dropout rate was lower. . . . A few
years ago student strikes were not often
threatened, faculties were not fearfully defensive.
. . . A few years ago there were no experimental
rabbinical schools.

Protestant, Catholic, and Jewish seminaries today have
the same motto: "Business as *un*-usual!"

Some Work on the System. There is a growing per-
ception among church reformers that it will do little good to
turn out a new-model parson for assignment to the same old
slots. Nor will it help much to retool and fix up the present
man on the job if he must labor with the same old expectations, well-worn ruts, and dreadful lack of tools and equipment.

Some of the "same old slots" in the same old system
that need reforming (just for a start) are: church management, clergy deployment, lay leadership, church member
relations, and organizational goals.

Management. For years, churches have recognized
the advantage of applying business techniques to fundraising,
and have called in experts to provide specialized advice.
Some have now begun to retain management specialists, such
as Consultation Search in the hope of pulling church operation
more into line with twentieth century business practices.

"There are many answers to church problems *already*, and many techniques available," says Chicago management consultant Richard S. Lopata, whose firm assists
businesses, hospitals, and churches. "The same knowledge applies to them all. We don't try to reshape organizations. We
just ask, 'What's your problem?' Tell us what you want to
do and where you want to go and we'll get you there."

Deployment. One of the worst of the same old slots is the maldistribution of clergy. Like the maldistribution of wealth, most of the clergy go to the fewest of the people; greatest need has the fewest resources. More than this, there is no ladder to climb. As we have seen, there is often nowhere to go for promotion or advancement. Most churches are "bottom rung"—few people, no money, no prestige.

The situation is not new. What counts now is that, with institutional religion well past its peak years of expansion, the situation will not get better automatically.

It is almost certain that a very great number of today's small, starveling congregations will die. Hundreds in fact do, each year, despite astonishing tenacity and exhausting struggles.

What can be done about it? One promising approach is the "cluster ministry"—the association, or merging, of too-small congregations under a team of pastors. This directly remedies the "corner grocery" approach: each little congregation struggling to support its own total, rival operation without enough resources to do the job.

The "cluster" approach has application to larger congregations as well. Any size and combination of parishes can get together for a more efficient use of funds and buildings and professional resources.

For the clergyman, this approach holds promise that there will be a "ladder" of career achievement, and that "ministry" will be redefined in terms of its specialized functions, releasing him from the present "generalist" mis-definition of his job.

Examples of this new approach are everywhere. One of the more celebrated is in Columbia, Maryland, a new planned community. There, facilities and staffing are on an interfaith basis. A cluster in Washington, D.C., is credited with preventing violence on one "poor people's march," an example of how the cluster can mobilize resources for community situations.

Lay Leadership and Initiative. The problem in most parishes, says Loren Mead, Episcopal rector from Chapel Hill, North Carolina, is that church problems are defined and planned by a bureau somewhere above, and then handed down to the local group. Says Mead: "A few eager clergy snap them up, but the vast majority of parishes continue operating as if the program had never been invented. National officers develop ulcers from defending them, while the parishes continue to resist them."

Convinced that the parish "is not only our chief potential resource, but the only starting point readily and widely available to the church," Mead designed and was authorized to carry out an experimental program of parish renewal, "Project Test Pattern." In thirteen experimental parishes across the country, teams of trained facilitators are assisting local church people to evolve their own process and program.

The underlying premise of the project is that taking clergy or laity out of the parish for retraining in an enabling, facilitating approach, will only frustrate them if the parish itself in mode and expectation remains in the old authoritarian/dependency pattern. Says Mead: "The *system* must be changed!"

His project now attempts to change it. The "test" refers to experimentation with different patterns of total parish reorientation, in the hope of developing models for more general use later on.

Thus, some denominations are willing to gamble a little on change.

Member Relations. "Project Test Pattern" also aims

to help people in churches learn how to relate openly and constructively. Many of the consultants to the projects, who have contracts with the participating congregations, are clergy with training in small-group methods. Training and accreditation for such consultancy is being developed through an interdenominational body called "ARABS"—the Association for Religion and Applied Behavioral Science, an organization of persons whose professional objective is "to participate with religious systems in the planning of individual, group and organizational change."

Mrs. Cynthia Wedel, the first woman president of the National Council of Churches, is a psychologist and an accredited trainer-member of the new ARABS organization, who in her new role is abetting this process.

Organizational Goals. Some who find "the heart of it" in the local congregations see that people have been so wrapped up in the sheer mechanics of organization—budgets and fund drives, replacements for offices, buildings, and program planning and maintenance—that they have literally lost touch with their goals. Hence the need to help laity take a fresh look at what they're about and where they are going. They may find that their actual activities have little to do with their aims.

"It is more difficult to see goals clearly in a voluntary association," consultant Lopata notes. "But goal setting is very important. Goals should be set down very carefully, very specifically." One plan for clarifying church goals, or revising them, is the "Vanguard Project" designed by Josiah R. Bartlett. It enables congregations systematically to explore the open-ended questions, "What does this church mean to me and where do I want it to go?" Once their goals are firmly conceived and established among themselves, they can move on to step six of the project, which translates goals into program, staff, and budget.

Some "Work" on Worship. Religion's value is precisely that it is conservative: of meanings, continuity, a sense of the changeless amid change. But every great religious reform has had as a central aim to bring enduring values into contemporary consciousness through contemporary modes of expression.

So today in all faiths, renewal shows itself in renewal of worship. Most spectacular, perhaps, is the Catholic Mass, translated into the vernacular, framed in jazz and folk music. Suddenly, people become aware how dull and dead their well-worn rituals are, in terms of religion as a moving, vital experience, and the church as a genuinely vital community.

Take, for example, the typical "worship service" in the average main-line church on any usual Sunday morning at eleven.

It is both passive and second-hand. Sometimes the sermon has no tie with reality. The service leaves little room except at its margins for the personal interchange of which community's fabric is woven.

Once, perhaps, it came closer, when the townsfolk of a settled community gathered from houses and farms to listen to the most exciting, and only available regular live show: the parson "rightly dividing the Scripture," and for a subsequent hour of Sunday-best sociability. But even this may be a romantic view. More realistic, perhaps, would be to say, that when religion still regulated behavior, churchgoing was a more lively community event, making up for its bad hymns and long sermons by its social function.

Many churches, still, are strapped into Grandma's corset, laced into yesteryear's order of service, yesteryear's ideas of sermonizing, and yesteryear's railway-coach seating plan sanctuary.

How much life, how much cordial community, can we expect from a service characterized by stiff pews, passive listening, white shirts for the men, gloves and little basic suits for the women, pre-packaged order of service (already printed, and badly), mechanical repetition of creeds most people simply don't believe, the heavy air of piosity, service synchronized with Sunday School, the leaders of the worship (minister, choir, readers) carefully rehearsed to "perform"? in short, spontaneity = bad taste.

To participate in many Protestant services, one must have sharp eyes and a quick grasp of words in small type, which the "responsive" readings and litanies put in your mouth. It helps if you can sight read music (and words at the same time), but one can hardly "swing" with a hymn, so riveted to the page.

Of course, the very last thing you are encouraged to do is say what, if anything, you feel, in your own words and gestures. Indeed, except in the "guided" meditation you are not encouraged even to free your own thoughts. The "moment of silence" is not trusted to be more than that, lest it make Muzak-conditioned people uneasy.

"Religious experience" is understood as that of receptor only: somebody tuned in, to be turned on by carefully calculated stimuli of very low voltage. Even the minister has but low investment in his own "order of service." For him its elements are reduced to garnish for his sermon theme. Thus the "old time religion" has become a feeble carbon copy. To any spirit-filled, with-it Christian, these are truly "God's frozen people."

Many services and settings deliberately curb the senses. This is epitomized in Whittier's hymn, cherished more for its dreamy tune than its blue-nosed lyrics:

Dear Lord and Father of mankind
Forgive our foolish ways.
Restore us to our rightful mind,
In purer lives they service find:
In deeper reverence, praise.

These are the concluding lines of one of the good gray Quakers' interminable poems, called "The Brewing of Soma." It records a shocked Puritan's reaction to an East Indian cult which used a brew named "soma" for the same purposes as certain American Indians use peyote, and our kids use pot. Today's youth are on the side of soma; at any rate they find Whittierism dull.

Part of the solution is to "unscrew the pew" and release the worshiper from the restraints and inhibition of the past. The mood is shifting, as minister Raines asserts: "from solemnity to celebration," where "much of the emphasis in the service is on participation by the people, rather than performance by the minister alone. Instead of the traditional pastoral prayer, the minister or a layman may stand up and ask the people to express their concerns. Instead of a sermon, there may be slides, film, lay drama, pop songs. This swinging style prevails in a small minority of congregations across the country, but it has the feel and face of the future. A new-time religion is breaking out."

The New Bottles

Forward-looking pastors and reform-minded staff are wheedling and pushing many congregations toward renewal, but there are significant do-it-yourself repairs going on at the grass roots level, where laity themselves are determined to break away from conventional patterns. One such venture is Congregation Solel, in suburban Phoenix, Arizona.

This congregation is one of a bold few trying to break with the temple-stereotype, which builds a spectacular edifice and enjoys a temple-blest fun and food filled social life. The four-year-old group, whose name means "prepare the way" or "pathfinder" is as serious as it is creative in devising new methods to understand and dramatize their rich, ancient heritage and its present-day relevance. Rabbis are wont to complain that few study that heritage: in this temple, the laymen prepare much of their own study material, and on Fridays, alternate study programs with the usual worship. A lay committee does the planning, coming up with such events as a Seder on the desert, to simulate the original Exodus experience.

The congregation, of young married couples mostly, has several social action projects going in the community.

Temple Solel rents quarters from the Camelback Presbyterian Church, in which both minister and rabbi have their offices. The liaison was contracted in part because of future cooperative possibilities: so different are the "pitch" and potential market of the two congregations that, they laughingly admit, they pose no threat to one another, and complement one another in keeping the building busy. They wanted also to break with the usual formula of set, high-pressure dues, and did so—with a balanced budget and, to date, a modest surplus.

A sharing, democratic, community spirit moves these people—as it kept them from affiliating with the big downtown temple, whose 1,100 families and 3,000 people "was just too much."

"Besides," says Betsy Buxer, their board secretary, "in a large temple, the rabbi is *the authority*, and that's that!" "We have a committee in every area, and can outvote our rabbi," says Valerie Richter, their recording secretary. "Even though he's sometimes right when we are wrong."

"We have a study 'theme' for the year, for everybody, so that children and parents, all of us, are learning and talking together. Last year, it was the first five books of the Bible. This year, it's Israel."

"They wanted something really exciting," said their first full-time rabbi, Jerrold Goldstein, "and the Temple is almost never accused of being boring. I did not do it for them. I helped them do what they wanted to do. They wanted to break with the rigidities which had emerged in the Reform tradition: a formal liturgy, the rabbi's lecture."

Morton Scult, the Temple Solel president, concludes: "We have, in our by-laws, set a three hundred fifty member-family limit, and we're against the traditional temple sisterhood, both for the same reason. Our people want to participate as couples, and as families. They want a genuine religious experience, which they feel they can get only in small groups, in which they can personally relate."

Another new model—actually as old as religion itself —shows itself in a widespread, fast-moving trend back to smallness and intimacy, to cells and fellowships, church-families and house-churches. In conscious opposition to success equated with bigness is the slogan "think small!"

In its own life, one denomination stumbled upon this accidentally. In 1948, the sparsely scattered Unitarians established a program of small, lay-led, do-it-yourself religious groups, for liberals without access to Unitarian churches. The aims and purposes of the program could hardly have been more modest: the creation of informal groups (only ten members necessary) unhampered by the usual responsibilities and machinery of church organization, to provide a minimal organizational base for isolated members wherever they might be.

To the astonishment of the denomination, this makeshift creation rocketed: by the end of 1966, Unitarian "fellowships" had been organized in every province of Canada, and in every state of the Union, including Hawaii and Alaska, with the single exception of Rhode Island, in which eight churches had been long established. By that time, 687 Unitarian fellowships had been organized, 342 more than the total number of Unitarian *churches* at the start of the program, and 389 more than the number of Universalist congregations which, in 1961, combined with Unitarianism to form a merged denomination.

Some of the fellowships dropped by the wayside; many grew far larger than the intended pattern; and seventy-four of them evolved into full fledged churches. At the present time well over half the active congregations in the denomination are these lay-led "fellowships" or churches grown from them.

Observers inside and out were at a loss to explain the "success" of the Unitarian fellowships. In not a few cases, where both were available, people chose to join a fellowship in preference to a church. At least part of the reason was the opportunity provided for a genuine small group religious experience. In its attempt to serve isolated sympathizers, and to extend itself, the denomination had unwittingly created a new institutional form, addressed to the unmet needs of large numbers of people.

The yearning for, and return to, the more intimate, intensive small religious cell of such disciplined Judaic groups as the Essenes, or recurrent Christian forms down the ages such as the mediaeval "friends of God" or John Wesley's "classes," has all over the world been growing apace: in house churches of England and Scotland, in *ilots de quartiers* of France and Switzerland, *Hauskreise* of Germany, and Bible study groups in Holland and Norway. In America, examples range from Christian-cell movements such as "Yoke-fellows" through the proliferation of Esalen-spawned growth centers and sensitivity groups, to religious communes and permanent communities.

Even the Establishment is doing some venturing of its own, and trying some new designs with the "Establishment Seal of Approval." The "Hatful of Peas" and the "Church on the Mall" are shopping-center ministries, both developed and supported by Presbyterian churches.

"Hatful of Peas" at the plush Town and Country shopping center in Phoenix, Arizona, grew out of the concern of the Presbyterian Board of Home Missions, the Phoenix Presbytery, and the session (board) of the Camelback United Presbyterian Church. It is now co-sponsored by Catholic, Protestant, and Jewish groups, and some civic groups also.

The minister, who does not push the clergy angle, calling himself "director" is Kent Organ, twenty-nine, a new-style cleric. He spent a full year preparing himself by getting acquainted with community resources (police, suicide- and crime-prevention, hospital, counseling, employment, youth and geriatric agencies, etc.).

The handout card says simply: "A place to relax— coffee, tea, cokes—help with hassles—draft counseling—arts and crafts—rap sessions—pastoral assistance, etc."

He and his team of twenty-one "regulars" and fifteen substitutes (all volunteers) offer help to anyone who wanders by in need of it: "Where do these people go for relief except to the shopping center?" Avant garde paperbacks, refreshments, conversation provide an easy lead in. Clients are mainly youth. "We don't tell people we're church-oriented," says a pert young hostess-volunteer, "unless we're pressed."

"Church on the Mall" at Plymouth Meeting (Philadelphia), Pennsylvania, has a psychiatric social worker, Janet Neer, on its team with Rev. Allan Kinloch. Kinloch says that people who would never go to a clinic are willing to bring their problems to a neighborhood center. A large part of their counseling is devoted to drugs.

GLEM, the Greater Lawrence Ecumenical Ministry, in Massachusetts, is a two-year-old inner-city ministry supported by four denominations, in a mill town having today a large Spanish-speaking population. The project includes a tutoring program (people from the suburbs help people in their homes), rehabilitating housing, organizing a newspaper to bring varied ethnic groups together, learning and responding to people's wants and needs.

Another model, an "advocate ministry" was developed by the Rev. William Smith, and sponsored by a "mission" United Church congregation in suburban Contra Costa County, California. Smith found people who agreed with him that, rather than accept the building lot (already provided) and go the conventional route, a more vital kind of church would be a "house church," providing a closer community for members, and asking an acceptance of individual obligation for responsible action upon the "sins of suburbia."

Smith's special assignment was to fill an advocate role at all county board of supervisors' meetings, articulating needs and issues as these rarely receive articulation in a "bedroom" community. "I made it clear I wasn't hostile," he says, "but also that I was *there* and watching. It had an amazing effect!"

It would be cheerful to report that Smith's congregation grew and grew. It didn't: to keep it going he became a "tent-maker"—as a teacher. Most suburbia-dwellers are not yet ready.

Vaster Vistas

Some in the church have caught a larger vision. Convinced that the job is too big to do piecemeal, they are prepared to undertake nothing less than a full scale remodeling on all fronts.

Such a vision, of an all-out ecumenical and worldwide review, prompted the calling of the Second Vatican Council. Four years of study and preparation went in to the sessions. A steady stream of research and findings has been flowing from it ever since.

Acting on and inspired by this call, elements of the Roman Church and of other Christian bodies have since moved ahead. Others, in fear and apprehension at what they began, have since retreated. But a wide door was opened.

Such a vision—on a much smaller scale—prompted the call to a "systems conference" at Yale University in February, 1970. This was initiated by the Department of Ministry, National Council of Churches, and the United Church of Christ, who invited representatives of all parts of the "system": seminary heads, judiciary executives, mission people, career development and continuing education personnel, black church leaders, pastors, ex-pastors, pastors' wives, laymen, researchers, seminary professors. The conference didn't get far toward its aims, but it was a long shot, idealistic try.

Another such vision, even bolder perhaps, was seen by the Reformed Church in America: it passed a resolution to consider going out of business altogether, in order to start all over again from scratch!

This is an extraordinarily exciting time in history. We are witnessing nothing less than the total restructuring of society, a large part of which is the restructuring of religion and its vehicle, the church.

Most of us watch the upheaval with confusion and apprehension. Most of those who have given their lives to the cause of religion in the church watch the transition with horror and infinite pain. What they see is the crumbling of certainty, the erosion of the cornerstones: creed and dogma, sacrament and symbol, ritual and belief. They see the sacred walls cracking: the toppling of authority, the rampant skepticism, the wholesale withdrawal of lieutenants and captains. They see it as the end of an era—which it is—and peer into the blackness of a churchless, religionless void.

But new bells are ringing! Not just in the steeples, but in the streets, and in many hearts. Green shoots are indeed pushing up through the cracks in the cold mossy floors. New wine is bubbling in a thousand new vineyards, and new bottles are taking shape to hold the new wine.

"Churchianity" may be dead, but religion is not.

Religion is as alive and kicking as it ever was. Now it seeks new channels and new forms.

Religion is being redistributed and rearranged. Before our eyes from our grandstand seats, we can see the shape of the church, the shape of "ministry" changing. Who would be bold enough, yet, to describe that new shape, to call the shots of where and how it will end?

Of one thing at least we can be certain: through the whole religious struggle of the moment runs a central theme: the quest for personhood in its fullest dimensions. This is the thread that links all of the issues together—clergy defections, clergy divorces, new marriages, new ministries. When the church begins to fulfill this freshly awakened longing in the hearts of its people: its clergy and its laity, it will have turned the corner. The new day will be on its way.

Death of religion? Death of the church? Steeples, stained glass, and gothic arches may vanish, along with the old-fashioned parson, but never have so many set their hands and hearts and minds to the building. Some of it will be jerry-built, to be sure—pieced and patched and taped together. But much of it will be solid, very solid.

ANNOTATED BIBLIOGRAPHY

ANNOTATED BIBLIOGRAPHY

Chapter One   The Clergy Rebellion

Information on church statistics, notoriously undependable, and not always up to date, can be found in the following:

JACQUET, CONSTANT H., ed., *Yearbook of American Churches.* (New York: Council Press, National Council of Churches, 1970.) The standard reference for church statistics. Though inadequate, it is the best overall source available. For trends, public opinion polls (Gallup, and others) are sometimes more helpful than figures released by church bodies. *Yearbook* cites them, also.

Official Catholic Directory. (New York: P. J. Kenedy and Sons, published annually.) Catholic statistics, e.g., number of nuns, seminarians, and so forth.

ROBERTSON, D. J., *Should the Churches Be Taxed?* (Philadelphia: The Westminster Press, 1968.) Discusses insurmountable difficulties in determining the staggering and incalculable extent of church wealth.

On clergy in transition:

GRAY, FRANCINE DU PLESSIX, *Divine Disobedience: Profiles in Catholic Radicalism.* (New York: Alfred A. Knopf, 1970.) A report on the priests at Emmaus House and long biographical sections on Daniel and Philip Berrigan and on Ivan Illich.

HADDEN, JEFFREY K., *The Gathering Storm in the Churches: The Widening Gap Between Clergy and Laymen.* (New York: Doubleday and Co., 1969.) Hadden compares clergy attitudes—from his own research —with those of laymen—from the research of others.

His conclusion is that clergy are frustrated by the conservatism of laymen. (He does not treat frustration of laity by conservatism of clergy, however. Few researchers do.)

MILLER, WILLIAM ROBERT, *Goodbye, Jehovah*. (New York: Avon Discus Books, 1968.) Useful brief treatment of such figures as Harvey Cox, Stephen Rose, Bill Boyd, John Robinson.

Among the popular books about rabbis, recommended by rabbis as authentic:

LEOKUM, ARKADY, *The Temple*. (New York: World Publishing Co., 1969.)

POTOK, CHAIM, *The Chosen*. (New York: Fawcett World Library, 1967.)

TARR, HERBERT, Heaven Help Us! (New York: Random House, 1968.)

Remarks of laity and clergy quoted in Chapter I are taken from the following:

Published sources

BARTLETT, JOSIAH R., *Report of the Unitarian Universalist Ministerial Shifts Study*. (Boston: Unitarian Universalist Association, 1969.)

CUNNEEN, SALLY, *Sex: Female; Religion: Catholic*. (New York: Holt, Rinehart and Winston, 1968.)

JUD, GERALD J., MILLS, EDGAR W., JR., AND BURCH, GENEVIEVE W., *Ex-Pastors: Why Men Leave the Ministry*. (Philadelphia: Pilgrim Press, 1970.)

O'BRIEN, JOHN A., *Why Priests Leave*. (New York: Hawthorn Books, 1969.)

Unpublished sources

Questionnaire replies collected by the writer and her husband, in the course of other research, and for other publications.

Data from interviews, correspondence, and conversation, in preparation for this manuscript.

Data from symposia, research meetings, and conferences.

Note that these unpublished sources, along with special papers, M.A. theses and Ph.D. dissertations, are resources throughout these chapters.

Chapter Two   Genesis of the Exodus: the Larger Context

Religion in the 1950's, some representative sources:

Annals of the American Academy of Political and Social Science, 1960. Religious trends issue, includes articles on membership, theology, etc.

GLAZER, NATHAN, *American Judaism*. (Chicago: University of Chicago Press, 1957.) Chapter VII is on "The Jewish Revival."

HERBERG, WILL, *Protestant-Catholic-Jew, An Essay in American Religious Sociology*. (New York: Doubleday and Co., 1955.)

MARTY, MARTIN, *The New Shape of American Religion*. (New York: Harper and Brothers, 1958.)

Religion in the 1960's, some representative sources:

BERTON, PIERRE, *The Comfortable Pew*. (Philadelphia: J. B. Lippincott Co., 1965.)

CLARKE, O. FIELDING, *For Christ's Sake*. (New York: Morehouse-Barlow, 1964.)

COX, HARVEY, *The Secular City*. (New York: The Macmillan Co., 1965.)

HAMILTON, WILLIAM, AND ALTIZER, THOMAS J. J., *Radical*

Theology and the Death of God. (Philadelphia: The Westminster Press, 1963.)

KILBOURN, WILLIAM, ed., *The Restless Church.* (Philadelphia: J. B. Lippincott Co., 1965.)

The "Religious Revival" controversy:

GLOCK, CHARLES Y., "The Religious Revival in America?" reprinted in GLOCK, CHARLES Y., AND STARK, RODNEY, *Religion and Society in Tension.* (Chicago: Rand McNally and Co., 1965.) The answer to the question depends upon the dimension one is measuring: church membership, attendance, saying of prayers, and so on. The book deals also with the "crisis of belief" and "the new denominationalism."

LIPSET, SEYMOUR M., *The First New Nation.* (New York: Basic Books, 1963.) Lipset holds that from the beginning America has had strong religious and secular traits.

PARSONS, TALCOTT, "The Pattern of Religious Organization in the United States," in *Daedalus* (Summer 1958.) Parsons contends that religion is being redefined, reconstituted, and redistributed throughout the society.

Other references:

ALLPORT, GORDON W., "The Religious Context of Prejudice," in *Journal for the Scientific Study of Religion* (Fall 1965.) One of Allport's many treatments of prejudice, this one relates to church affiliation and the paradox of bigoted "Christians."

BERGER, PETER, *The Noise of Solemn Assemblies.* (Garden City, N.Y.: Doubleday and Co., 1961.) The relevance of the church is its irrelevance.

DAVIES, A. POWELL, *America's Real Religion.* (Boston: Beacon Press, 1949.) An early statement about America's diffused and outside-the-church religion. Others writing about this consensual "culture religion" include John C.

Bennett, Roy A. Eckhardt, W. Lloyd Warner, and, more recently, Robert Bellah, on "civil religion."

DEMERATH, N. J., III, AND HAMMOND, PHILLIP E., *Religion in Social Context: Tradition and Transition.* (New York: Random House, 1969.) Helpful summary of background and theory in sociology of religion and contemporary institutional issues.

DUGGAN, ROBERT, "Critical Issues in the Parish Ministry." (New York: paper distributed by Department of Ministry, National Council of Churches, 1969.)

HADDEN, JEFFREY K., *The Gathering Storm in the Churches: The Widening Gap Between Clergy and Laymen.* (New York: Doubleday and Co., 1969.) Has a major section on the "crisis of belief."

HARRISON, PAUL, *Authority and Power in the Free Church Tradition. A Social Case Study of the American Baptist Convention.* (Princeton: Princeton University Press, 1959.) Even a "free" church, based on autonomous congregations, tends to gravitate toward bureaucratic patterns.

LECKY, ROBERT S., AND WRIGHT, H. ELLIOTT, *Can These Bones Live? The Failure of Church Renewal.* (New York: Sheed and Ward, 1969.) Good summary of recent attempts at renewal. The authors are disheartened at those results.

NEUSNER, JACOB, "Radical Judaism," in "Does Religion Have a Future?" a collation of articles by religious leaders, in *The Ladies' Home Journal*, December 1969.

STARK, RODNEY, AND GLOCK, CHARLES Y., *American Piety: The Nature of Religious Commitment.* (Berkeley: University of California Press, 1968.) An examination of trends in religious belief in America, based on two samples: their own survey of 3,000 church members of all faiths, in four counties of northern California, and a National Opinion Research Council sample of 1,976 adults of all faiths, church and non-church members, from across the country.

Chapter Three   Halfway Houses for Runaway Clergy

Most of the resources for this chapter are unpublished. (See unpublished sources, above, Bibliography for Chapter I.) Quotations from directors and other agency personnel are largely from interviews on location, supplemented by agency reports and releases, staff-written articles, and organization newsletters.

> *New Focus: For Church Alumni and Those on the "Inside Edge."* (Santa Barbara, California: Bishop Pike Foundation, bi-monthly.)

Other resources for this chapter:

> BARTLETT, JOSIAH R., *Report of the Unitarian Universalist Ministerial Shifts Study.* (Boston: Unitarian Universalist Association, 1969.)

> COVELL, DAVID R., JR., *Satisfaction and Dissatisfaction Among Parish Priests: A Preliminary Discussion.* (New York: Executive Council of the Episcopal Church, June 1970.) The first of several "preliminary" reports of a three-phase Episcopal survey, begun in July 1968. It included thirteen percent of all active parish clergy: 913 priests, their wives, and 2,400 vestry members.

> DILLON, VALERIE VANCE, "Bearings: Serving Troubled Servants of the Lord," in *The Sign,* June 1969. Includes cases of Bearings' clients.

> DONAHOE, MICHAEL, AND BLUE, EARL, *The Earl Blue Report on Clergy Disaffection.* (San Francisco: Earl Blue Associates, 1970.) Report of a vocational placement firm based solely on its own clients and correspondents, persons who had already left the active ministry or were contemplating doing so.

> FICHTER, JOSEPH, *America's Forgotten Priests: What They Are Saying.* (New York: Harper and Row, 1968.) One of the many post-Vatican II research spinoffs. Report of a neglected and rarely heard from category of priest, the diocesan priest, by a prominent research sociologist.

JUD, GERALD J., MILLS, EDGAR W., JR., AND BURCH, GENEVIEVE W., *Ex-Pastors: Why Men Leave the Ministry.* (Philadelphia: Pilgrim Press, 1970.)

O'BRIEN, JOHN A., *Why Priests Leave.* (New York: Hawthorn Books, 1969.)

Chapter Four   Second Oldest Profession

BLIZZARD, SAMUEL, "The Minister's Dilemma," in the *Christian Century*, April 25, 1956. Report of research which focused clergy on role conflict.

CARLIN, J. E., AND MENDLOVITZ, S. H., "The American Rabbi: A Religious Specialist Responds to a Lack of Authority," in SKLARE, MARSHALL, *The Jews.* (Glencoe, Ill.: The Free Press, 1958.) One of many articles which wrestle with clerical role problems; this one, in the Jewish context.

DEMERATH, N. J., III, AND HAMMOND, PHILLIP E., *Religion in Social Context: Tradition and Transition.* (New York: Random House, 1969.) The concluding section summarizes the problems of integration *vs.* prophecy in the church.

GLASSE, JAMES D., *Profession: Minister.* (Nashville: Abingdon Press, 1968.) Systematic review of literature and clergy problems. Glasse's aim is to minister to clergy identity problems. He rejects some stereotypes, such as anti-professionalism and the "generalist" concept; but while the clergy image changes, he himself falls into stereotyped usage; for example, he deals with parish *as* ministry.

GLOCK, CHARLES Y., RINGER, BENJAMIN B., AND BABBIE, EARL R., *To Comfort and to Challenge: A Dilemma of the Contemporary Church.* (Berkeley: University of California Press, 1967.) One of many treatments of the perennial tension between contradictory aims of religious institutions: comforting and supporting people, and challenging and changing them and society. Based on a survey of Episcopal clergy and laity, and their respective expectations.

WEBER, MAX, *The Sociology of Religion*, trans. Ephraim Fischoff. (Boston: Beacon Press, 1963.) Only a fragment of Weber's monumental comparative work on religious institutions. It was he who first analyzed the function of charisma in religious development, and its routinization in the subsequent process of bureaucratization.

YINGER, J. MILTON, *Religion in the Struggle for Power. A Study in the Sociology of Religion.* (Durham, N.C.: Duke University Press, 1946.) An early treatment of the pulling and hauling in the institutional church, between idealism and prophecy on the one hand, and maintenance and influence on the other.

Chapter Five   The Other Revolution

ARGYLE, MICHAEL, *Religious Behavior.* American edition. (Glencoe, Ill.: The Free Press, 1959.) A summary of British and American studies of religious institutions. Includes research findings in re: sex as a factor in church membership and participation.

CULVER, ELSIE T., *Women in the World of Religion.* (New York: Doubleday and Co., 1967.) Summarizes status of women in official roles in Christian churches.

CUNNEEN, SALLY, *Sex: Female; Religion: Catholic.* (New York: Holt, Rinehart and Winston, 1968.) Report of a survey of attitudes by Catholic women as they relate to the church.

DALY, MARY, *The Church and the Second Sex.* (New York: Harper and Row, 1968.)

GIBSON, ELSIE, *When the Minister Is a Woman.* (New York: Holt, Rinehart and Winston, 1970). Based on actual cases.

GRANT, DOROTHY S., *Universalism in Iowa, 1830–1963.* (Des Moines: Prairie State Unitarian Universalist Association,

1964.) One chapter of church history in which clergy women figured prominently.

KLOETZLI, WALTER, *The City Church: Death or Renewal?* (Philadelphia: Muhlenberg Press, 1961.) A study of eight urban Lutheran congregations. An "afterword" by Charles Y. Glock, "A Sociologist Looks at the Parish Church," puts these findings into the context of religious research generally, including the place of women in the church.

SCOTT, CLINTON LEE, *The Universalist Church of America: A Short History*. (Boston: Universalist Historical Society, 1957.)

Quotations from and about women in the church were taken from the following:

Published sources:

Report of the Committee on Goals. (Boston: Unitarian Universalist Association, 1967.)

CUNNEEN, SALLY (see above).

JUD, GERALD J., MILLS, EDGAR W., AND BURCH, GENEVIEVE W., *Ex-Pastors: Why Men Leave the Ministry*. (Philadelphia: Pilgrim Press, 1970.)

SHEA, TERENCE, "Two Seek to End Age-Old Sex Barriers in Ministry," in *The National Observer*, March 30, 1970. The cases of Betty Schiess and Sally Priesand.

"The Woman Minister in a Liberal Denomination," in *The Bridge*, magazine of the Unitarian Universalist Women's Federation, May, 1970. The first article of a series on women ministers in this denomination.

Unpublished sources:

NEAL, SISTER MARIE AUGUSTA, S.N.D., director of "The Sisters Survey" sponsored by the Conference of Major Superiors of Women Religious in the U.S. (CMSW) in 1965. An unprecedented several-stage research project to determine the degree of readiness for change on the

part of Catholic women's orders. 139,000 of the 150,000
sisters polled, a ninety-two percent response, replied to a
649-item questionnaire. Results are still being tabulated.

————, unpublished research on 396 health, education,
and welfare orders, and a brief study of contemplative
orders (both women's orders).
See, also, unpublished sources in bibliography for Chapter
One, above.

Chapter Six   Holy Matrimony

DOUGLAS, WILLIAM, *Ministers' Wives*. (New York: Harper
and Row, 1965.) One of the few studies of ministers'
wives. Research report on 6,000 wives of thirty-seven
denominations.

HERMAND, PIERRE, *The Priest: Celibate or Married?*
(Baltimore: Helicon Press, 1965.) An early treatment of
a subject with a rapidly growing literature. This presents
the case against celibacy, a good summary of problems
relating thereto.

LEA, HENRY CHARLES, *An Historical Sketch of Sacerdotal
Celibacy in the Christian Church*. (Boston: Houghton
Mifflin Co., 1884.)

LE BLANC, ARTHUR, "I'm Not Lonely Now," in O'BRIEN,
JOHN, *Why Priests Leave*. (New York: Hawthorn Books,
1969.) One of twelve "intimate stories" of priests who
have left the church over the celibacy issue. All are
pro-celibacy reform.

SANDERS, JOSEPH, S.J., "Celibacy and the Declining Rate
of Membership in the Society of Jesus." (Boston: Boston
College, unpublished manuscript, Fall 1969.) An attempt
to explain the decline in Jesuit membership, with special
exploration of the celibacy issue. A review of the history
of celibacy and its literature, the pros and cons. This
priest-sociologist concludes that celibacy is not the major
factor in Jesuit departures. It may, however, be more of an
obstacle for young men who contemplate entering.

SMITH, CHARLES MERRILL, *How To Become a Bishop
Without Being Religious*. (New York: Doubleday and

Co., 1965.) Comment on this book by Demerath and Hammond, *op. cit.*, p. 237: "Trenchant satire that illuminates painlessly what many sociologists have said so painfully."

Unpublished sources: interviews, questionnaires as above (see Chapter One bibliography.)

In this chapter, questionnaires from the following study were used:

BARTLETT, JOSIAH R., *Report of Unitarian Universalist Ministerial Shifts Study*. (Boston: Unitarian Universalist Association, 1969.) This study looked at major "life shifts" of clergy over a five-year period (1964–1968). Life shifts were defined as: moving out of parish, moving out of ministry, obtaining final divorce. The research design included three questionnaires for wives:
- one for wives of clergy who had left the parish, or left the ministry altogether
- one for wives of clergy still in the parish
- one for ex-wives; those whose divorce was final.

Such a prominent focus on marital context is unusual in studies of clergy departures. It finds a close connection between marriage and career in the ministry.

Chapter Seven   The Case of the Vanishing Parson

MENGES, ROBERT J., AND DITTES, JAMES E., *Psychological Studies of Clergymen: Abstracts of Research*. (New York: Thomas Nelson and Sons, 1965.) An inventory of approximately 700 separate "psychological studies of clergymen" of all faiths and at all levels of academic sophistication. The field is in rapid growth and flux. Supplement is pending.

SMITH, CHARLES MERRILL, *How to Become a Bishop Without Being Religious*. (New York: Doubleday and Co., 1965.) A tongue-in-check summary of clerical stereotypes.

SUPER, DONALD E., *The Psychology of Careers*. (New York: Harper and Row, 1957.) The theory upon which

the Northeast Career Center operates: "a
career-development concept very appropriate to the
needs of church professionals."

Unpublished sources:

The main sources used in this chapter are personal
interviews. In addition, several papers:

BROWN, THOMAS E., "Occupational Counseling as a Way
to Assist Church Professionals in Development of
Leadership Capability." Position statement by the
director of the Center. (Princeton, N.J.: Northeast
Career Center, 1969. Mimeographed.)

CHICHESTER, HELON, "Displaced Persons Are Deprived
Persons." Unpublished paper. (Berkeley, California,
Church Divinity School of the Pacific, n.d.) An inquiry
into the present situations of this Episcopal school's
alumni who "have elected to leave the more typical
parochial ministry." Interviews and open-ended questions
of more than sixty graduates.

TUCKER, GRAYSON, *History and Development of the
Northeast Career Center in Princeton, New Jersey.*
(Unpublished thesis, Louisville Presbyterian Seminary,
Summer 1969.) The purpose of the study is ". . . to
consider a pattern whereby a similar process may be
initiated during the seminary years of a minister's
professional career."

Chapter Eight   The Called and the Calling

In addition to the sources, published and unpublished, cited above,
this chapter draws on the following:

Published sources:

BRIDSTON, K. R. AND CULVER, D. W., *Pre-Seminary Education.*
(Minneapolis: Augsburg Publishing House, 1965.)

"Drop-Outs," in *Tomorrow.* (New York: The Ministers
and Missionaries Benefit Board of the American Baptist
Convention, May 1969.) A special issue on the problem

of ministerial dropouts from the American Baptist
Convention. Some statistics on these former ministers.

LEIFFER, MURRAY H., *Changing Expectations and Ethics in
the Professional Ministry. A Research Report on the
Attitudes of Ministers in Five Protestant Denominations.*
(Evanston, Illinois: Garrett Theological Seminary, 1969.)
The denominations involved were United Methodist,
United Presbyterian, Southern Baptist, Presbyterian U.S.,
United Church of Christ.

MILLS, EDGAR W., "Career Change in the Protestant
Ministry," in *Ministry Studies*, III, 1, May, 1969. (New
York: Department of Public Services, National Council
of Churches.) A digest of his own in-depth analysis of
sixty present and former United Presbyterian parish
ministers. (A Harvard Ph.D. thesis, 1966, originally
published as Monograph #46 in the Harvard Studies in
Career Development.) All issues of *Ministry Studies* are
relevant and suggest additional materials and resources.

"Report of the Temporary Commission on Continuing
Education," *Blue Book, Part III*, 181st General Assembly
of the United Presbyterian Church in the United States
of America. (Philadelphia: Office of the General
Assembly, 1969.) Report of a three-year study by a
blue-ribbon commission, spelling out the "problem that
occasions the need for a church-wide approach to
continuing education, a proposed program, a structure
and strategy."

WELSH, CLEMENT, *Concepts in Continuing Education for
Ministry: A Position Paper.* (New York: Executive
Council of the Episcopal Church, 1969.) A position paper
commended to the Episcopal Church for its
consideration. Contains references and available resources
on continuing education for ministry, including
conference proceedings, and so forth.

Unpublished sources:

BALDWIN, PETER, "Vocational Values of One Hundred
Unitarian Ministers." Ph.D. dissertation. (Boston: Boston
University Graduate School, 1964.) A content analysis

of current concepts of liberal ministry and the role of the liberal church, from statements of ministers seeking placement.

BARTLETT, JOSIAH R., "Expectations and Realizations in the Parish Ministry." (Unitarian Universalist Association, 1969.) Comparison of ministerial realizations (from questionnaire responses of clergy who entered the ministry: 1961–1965) with expectations (statements by same clergy on entering.)

CRANE, JOHN A., "Conflicting Demands in the Personal Life of the Minister." Paper prepared for Pacific Coast Unitarian Ministers Association meeting, Merlin, Oregon, 1961.

EASTER, WILLIAM, designer of Resources Center for Parish Clergy, Lubbock, Texas. Report of 600 interviews with former clergy, and persons working with them, across the country, also given as four theme talks for the Conference on the Shape of Clergy Restlessness. (Cambridge, Mass., January 1970, sponsored jointly by the Boston Theological Institute and the Episcopal Theological School.)

FOULKES, ROBERT G., "The Career Development Council." (Undated mimeographed report to the General Council of the United Presbyterian Church.)

GILLILAN, HUGH W., "A Study of Former Unitarian Universalist Ministers." Ph.D. dissertation. (Salt Lake City: University of Utah, June 1970.) The findings confirm those of other studies: United Church of Christ, Presbyterian, Unitarian Universalist, and so forth.

HAVERSAT, ALBERT L., *Statistical Report: Lutheran Church of America Ministers Who Have Been Removed from the Register of Active Ministers* (Sept. 15, 1962–October 10, 1968). (New York: Board of Theological Education, Lutheran Church of America.)

KATZ, ROBERT L., *The Future of the Rabbinate–Ascribed vs. Achieved Leadership.* Perspectives from Sociology. (Cincinnati: Hebrew Union College, now in press.)

LOWERY, JAMES L., JR., *Small Congregations and Their Clergy* (A Partial Study of the 1967–1968 Situation in the Episcopal Church in the United States with Some Recommendations.) (Boston: Harvard Divinity School, January 1970.)

Chapter Nine   Conclusion: New Bells and New Bottles

The following are additional resources, not listed previously:

Published sources:

BARTLETT, LAILE E., *Bright Galaxy: Ten Years of Unitarian Fellowships.* (Boston: Beacon Press, 1960.) The first of several publications by this writer on the return to the small religious group movement.

BARTLETT, JOSIAH R., AND LAILE E., *Moment of Truth: An Analysis of Unitarian Universalism.* (Berkeley: privately published, 1968.) Chapter VI looks at "Sunday morning at eleven." Other chapters consider other aspects of institutional religion: changing ministry, seminaries, religious education.

COVELL, DAVID R., JR., "Annex to the Interim Report." (New York: Executive Council of the Episcopal Church, June 1970.) Research findings on Episcopal clergy deployment.

FRAY, HAROLD R., JR., *Conflict and Change in the Church.* (Philadelphia: Pilgrim Press, 1969.) Conflict management in one parish (United Church of Christ, Newton, Mass.)

GLOCK, CHARLES Y., AND STARK, RODNEY, *Christian Beliefs and Anti-Semitism.* (New York: Harper and Row, 1966.) The case against the church: report of research findings which correlate "most Christian" with "most anti-semitic."

GUSTAFSON, JAMES, *Treasure in Earthen Vessels, The Church as a Human Community.* (New York: Harper and Row, 1961.) A plea for, and examination of, the church as an institution among other institutions.

ISRAEL, RICHARD J., "The New Morality and the Rabbis,"

in *Conservative Judaism*, XXIV, 1, Fall 1969. Ancient tradition in the contemporary conflict. Cited as one of many attempts to relate clerical patterns to changing mores.

JUD, GERALD J., *Pilgrim's Process*. (Philadelphia: United Church Press, 1967.) A sermon, really, by a church executive to his own people in their local churches, urging flexibility and openness to change. Cited as an example of "establishment men" who are pushing for change. Jud was a moving spirit in the Yale Systems Conference (1970).

KIRK, DAVID, compiler, *Quotations from Chairman Jesus*. (Springfield, Illinois: Templegate Publishers, 1969.) One of many releases from the Emmaus House community, of which David Kirk is spokesman. Another, their quarterly, *The Bread Is Rising*, strikingly capsules the spirit of the community.

MARNEY, CARLYLE, "The New Breed's Man." (New York: The Ministers and Missionaries Benefit Board, American Baptist Convention, 1967.) This address, by the moving spirit of Interpreter's House, Lake Junaluska, N.C., suggests the approach of the new clergy-help agencies and personnel.

NEAL, SISTER MARIE AUGUSTA, S.N.D., *Values and Interests in Social Change*. (Englewood Cliffs, N.J.: Prentice-Hall, 1965.) Report of a sociological study of diocesan clergy in the Archdiocese of Boston. The book is theoretically oriented. In addition to its aim of developing a satisfactory model for measuring social change—in as tenuous a realm as values—it explores readiness for change among parish priests.

Rabbinic training: "The Future of Rabbinic Training in America: A Symposium," in *Judaism: A Quarterly Journal* (New York: American Jewish Congress, Fall 1969.) The proceedings of a symposium sponsored by *Judaism*. Includes opinion from all branches of contemporary Judaism: Reform, Orthodox, Conservative,

Reconstructionist; and from all elements: student, faculty, active rabbi, independent scholar.

RAINES, ROBERT, "The New-Time Religion," in *Ladies' Home Journal* collation "Does Religion Have a Future?" (December 1969.) One of a collection of suggestive projections of religion in the future. Another is "The Gospel of Cluster 39," a forecast of churches as small-group, encounter-type religion, by Sam Keen, former Presbyterian seminary professor now at the Center for Studies of the Person, La Jolla, California.

WESTBERG, GRANGER, "An American Academy of Parish Clergy: Why Not?" in the *Christian Century*, April 28, 1965. The suggestion from which the American Academy of Parish Clergy sprang.

Unpublished sources:

Sources for persons and organizations cited in this chapter are, in the main, unpublished, consisting largely of interviews. These are supplemented by personal papers, poetry, organizational releases, progress reports, and working papers obtained at the locations themselves.